# WORLD ENGLISH 2

## THIRD EDITION

Real People · Real Places · Real Language

Kristin L. Johannsen and Rebecca Tarver Chase, Authors

D1603927

**NATIONAL GEOGRAPHIC**
L E A R N I N G

Australia · Brazil · Mexico · Singapore · United Kingdom · United States

**NATIONAL GEOGRAPHIC**
**LEARNING**

National Geographic Learning,
a Cengage Company

**World English Level 2: Real People, Real Places,
Real Language, Third Edition**
**Kristin L. Johannsen and Rebecca Tarver Chase,
Authors**

Publisher: Sherrise Roehr

Executive Editor: Sarah Kenney

Senior Development Editor: Margarita Matte

Media Researcher: Leila Hishmeh

Senior Technology Product Manager:
  Lauren Krolick

Director of Global Marketing: Ian Martin

Senior Product Marketing Manager:
  Caitlin Thomas

Heads of Regional Marketing:
  Charlotte Ellis (Europe, Middle East, and Africa)
  Kiel Hamm (Asia)
  Irina Pereyra (Latin America)

Production Manager: Daisy Sosa

Manufacturing Planner: Mary Beth Hennebury

Art Director: Brenda Carmichael

Operations Support: Hayley Chwazik-Gee

Compositor: MPS Limited

For permission to use material from this text or product,
submit all requests online at **cengage.com/permissions**
Further permissions questions can be emailed to
**permissionrequest@cengage.com**

World English 2 ISBN: 978-0-357-11367-7
World English 2 + MyWorldEnglishOnline ISBN: 978-0-357-13021-6

**National Geographic Learning**
20 Channel Center Street
Boston, MA 02210
USA

Locate your local office at **international.cengage.com/region**

Visit National Geographic Learning online at **ELTNGL.com**
Visit our corporate website at www.cengage.com

Printed in China by RRD
Print Number: 04      Print Year: 2020

Thank you to the educators who provided invaluable feedback during the development of the third edition of the *World English* series:

## AMERICAS

### Brazil

**Gabriely Billordo,** Berlitz, Porto Alegre
**Bruna Caltabiano,** Caltabiano Idiomas, Sao Paulo
**Sophia de Carvalho,** Inglês Express, Belo Horizonte
**Renata Coelho,** 2b English for you, Florianopolis
**Rebecca Ashley Hibas,** Inglês Express, Belo Horizonte
**Cristina Kobashi,** Cultivar Escola de Idiomas, Guaratinguetá
**Silvia Teles Barbosa,** Colégio Cândido Portinari, Salvador

### Chile

**Jorge Cuevas,** Universidad Santo Tomás, Los Angeles

### Colombia

**Ruben Cano,** UPB University, Medellin
**Javier Vega,** Fundación Universitaria de Popayán, Popayán

### Costa Rica

**Jonathan Acuna,** Centro Cultural Costarricense Americano, San José
**Lilly Sevilla,** Centro Cultural Costarricense Americano, San José

### Mexico

**Jose Aguirre,** Instituto Tecnológico Superior de Irapuato, Salamanca
**Alejandro Alvarado Cupil,** Instituto Tecnológico de Minatitlán, Minatitlan
**Jhosellin Angeles,** ITSOEH, Mixquiahuala de Juárez, Hidalgo
**René Bautista,** BUAP, Puebla
**Imelda Félix,** Colegio Cervantes Costa Rica, Guadalajara
**Isabel Fernández,** Universidad Autónoma de Aguascalientes, Aguascalientes
**Andres Garcia,** FES Aragon (UNAM), Mexico City
**Jessica Garcia,** Colegio Cultural, Puebla
**Lazaro Garcia,** Tecnológico de Toluca, Metepec
**Fernando Gómez,** Universidad Tecnológica Jalisco,Guadalajara
**Alma Gopar,** FES Zaragoza (UNAM), Mexico City
**Inés Gutierrez,** University of Colima, Colima
**Jesus Chavez Hernandez,** Universidad Aeronáutica en Querétaro, Colón
**Cristina Mendez,** Instituto Tecnológico Superior de Irapuato, Irapuato
**Elena Mioto,** UNIVA, Guadalajara
**Rubén Mauricio Muñoz Morales,** Universidad Santo Tomás, Villavicencio
**Maria Rodríguez,** Universidad Aeronáutica en Querétaro, Colón
**Ana Lilia Terrazas,** ICO, Puebla

### United States

**Amy Fouts,** Face to Face Learning Center, Doral, FL
**Virginia Jorge,** UCEDA International, New Brunswick, NJ
**Richard McDorman,** Language On, Miami, FL
**Sarah Mikulski,** Harper College, Palatine, IL
**Rachel Scheiner,** Seattle Central College, Seattle, WA
**Pamela Smart-Smith,** Virginia Tech Language and Culture Institute, Blacksburg, VA
**Marcie Stone,** American English College, Rowland Heights, CA
**Colin Ward,** Lone Star College-North Harris, Houston, TX
**Marla Yoshida,** University of California, Irvine, CA

## ASIA

**Nazarul Azali,** UiTM Cawangan Melaka, Alor Gajah
**Steven Bretherick,** Tohoku Fukushi University, Sendai
**Sam Bruce,** Soka University, Hachioji
**Karen Cline-Katayama,** Hokusei Gakuen University and Tokai University, Sapporo
**Tom David,** Japan College of Foreign Languages, Tokyo
**Johnny Eckstein,** Soka University, Hachioji
**Meg Ellis,** Kyoto Tachibana University, Kyoto
**Thomas Goetz,** Hokusei Gakuen University, Sapporo
**Katsuko Hirai,** Matsuyama University, Matsuyama
**Paul Horness,** Soka University, Hachioji
**David Kluge,** Nanzan University, Nagoya
**Stephen Lambacher,** Aoyama Gakuin University, Tokyo
**Yi-An Lin,** National Taipei University of Business, Taipei
**Kerry McCatty,** Soka University, Hachioji
**Gregg McNabb,** Shizuoka Institute of Technology, Shizuoka
**Collin Mehmet,** Matsumoto University, Matsumoto City
**Sean Mehmet,** Shinshu University, Matsumoto
**Lin Mingying,** Soka University, Hachioji
**Erika Nakatsuka,** Soka University, Hachioji
**Seiko Oguri,** Chubu University, Nagoya
**Thomas Nishikawa,** Ritsumeikan University, Kyoto
**Sean Otani,** Tottori University, Tottori
**Daniel Paller,** Kinjo Gakuin University, Nagoya
**Tomomi Sasaki,** Ibaraki University, Mito
**Mark Shrosbree,** Tokai University, Hiratsuka
**Brent Simmons,** Aichi Gakuin University, Nagoya
**Mikiko Sudo,** Soka University, Hachioji
**Monika Szirmai,** Hiroshima International University, Hiroshima
**Matthew Taylor,** Kinjo Gakuin University, Nagoya
**James Thomas,** Kokusai Junior College, Tokyo
**Asca Tsushima,** Soka University, Hachioji
**Hui Chun Yu,** Macau University of Science and Technology, Macau

| Listening | Speaking and Pronunciation | Reading | Writing | Video Journal |
|---|---|---|---|---|
| General and Focused Listening<br><br>An Interview:<br><br>Rice Farming | Comparing Diets<br><br>Discussing Types of Food<br><br>Linking Words Together | The Paleo Diet: Natural and Healthy? | Writing Main Ideas and Supporting Details | **Wide Awake Bakery**<br><br>This National Geographic Short Film Showcase video describes how baking delicious bread can change your life. |
| General and Focused Listening<br><br>Conversations:<br><br>Small Talk | Talking about Yourself<br><br>Starting a Conversation<br><br>*Have* or *Has* vs. Contractions | Endangered Languages | Giving Examples | **Marie's Dictionary**<br><br>This National Geographic Short of the Week video describes Marie's efforts to archive her native Wukchumni language and save her language and culture for others. |
| General and Focused Listening<br><br>A Radio Interview:<br><br>Jardin Nomade in Paris | Discussing the Future of Your City<br><br>Describing the Pros and Cons of Cities<br><br>Stressed Syllables Before *-tion* Suffix | Streets for People | Writing a Paragraph With a Good Topic Sentence | **How to Reinvent the Apartment Building**<br><br>In this TED Talk, Moshe Safdie talks about reinventing high-rise apartment buildings and making them better. |
| Focused Listening<br><br>Discussions:<br><br>Different Lifestyles | Talking about Staying Healthy<br><br>Suggesting Easy Remedies<br><br>Linking with the Comparative and Superlative | Attitude Is Everything | Writing a Paragraph Using Supporting Details | **Living Beyond Limits**<br><br>In this TED Talk, Amy Purdy explains how obstacles can help us be creative. |
| General and Focused Listening<br><br>An Interview:<br><br>Dr. Jenny Daltry: Wildlife Conservationist and Ecologist | Discussing Challenges<br><br>Talking about Abilities<br><br>Words That End in *-ed* | Making a Difference: Bali | Writing a Paragraph about a Challenging Experience | **Success Story: Recycling in the Philippines**<br><br>In this National Geographic video, we learn how communities in the Philippines created a solution for discarded plastic fishing nets. |
| General and Focused Listening<br><br>Conversation:<br><br>Becoming an Adult | Talking about Events in Your Life<br><br>Getting More Information<br><br>The Schwa Sound /ə/ in Unstressed Syllables | Innovation in Africa | Writing a Paragraph to Describe a Life Transition | **The Magic Washing Machine**<br><br>In this TED Talk, Hans Rosling explains the incredible effect a simple machine can have on our lives. |

| Listening | Speaking and Pronunciation | Reading | Writing | Video Journal |
|---|---|---|---|---|
| General and Focused Listening<br>Discussions:<br>Needs and Wants | Discussing Spending Habits<br>Talking about Priorities<br>Content vs. Function Words | A Zero-Waste Lifestyle | Writing about Your Future Life | **The Dogist**<br>In this National Geographic Short Film Showcase video, Elias Weiss Friedman explains how he finds happiness while taking photos of dogs. |
| General and Focused Listening<br>A Radio Program:<br>The Bluefin Tuna | Talking about Issues That Affect Nature and Their Consequences<br>Talking about Protecting Animals<br>Phrases in Sentences | Making a Difference: Small Changes | Writing a Paragraph about an Environmental Issue | **Life Lessons from Big Cats**<br>In this TED Talk, Beverly and Dereck Joubert explain how getting to know the personalities of big cats can help protect Africa. |
| General and Focused Listening<br>A Talk:<br>The Sami People | Comparing Life Now and in the Past<br>Discussing How Things Used to Be in the Past<br>Reduction of *Used to* | The Silk Routes | Writing a Paragraph on One of the New 7 Wonders of the World | **Searching for Genghis Khan**<br>This National Geographic Learning video describes how Albert Lin uses the power of technology and the contributions of non-scientists in the search for historical sites. |
| General and Focused Listening<br>Conversations:<br>Vacations | Discussing Preparing for a Trip<br>Describing Things You Do at the Airport<br>Reduction of *have to* and *has to* | Four Reasons Why Traveling Is Good for You | Writing a Travel Blog | **Why Art Thrives at Burning Man**<br>In this TED Talk, Nora Atkinson describes how curiosity and engagement are inspired by this art festival. |
| General and Focused Listening<br>An Interview:<br>A Restaurant Owner in Thailand | Discussing Career Choices<br>Talking about Career Planning<br>Intonation in Questions | Changing Careers | Writing a Personal Profile | **Joel Sartore: The Photo Ark**<br>In this National Geographic video, Joel Sartore talks about his work documenting animal species. |
| General and Focused Listening<br>Discussions:<br>Local Celebrations or Holidays | Describing Celebrations<br>Expressing Congratulations and Good Wishes<br>Question Intonation with Lists | The Rituals of Life Events | Writing a Substantiated Opinion | **Dance of the Flyers: Jacinta's Journey**<br>In this National Geographic Short Film Showcase video, Jacinta describes her journey as the first female flyer in Mexico. |

# Food for Life

Harvester works in high-density tomato greenhouse in the Netherlands.

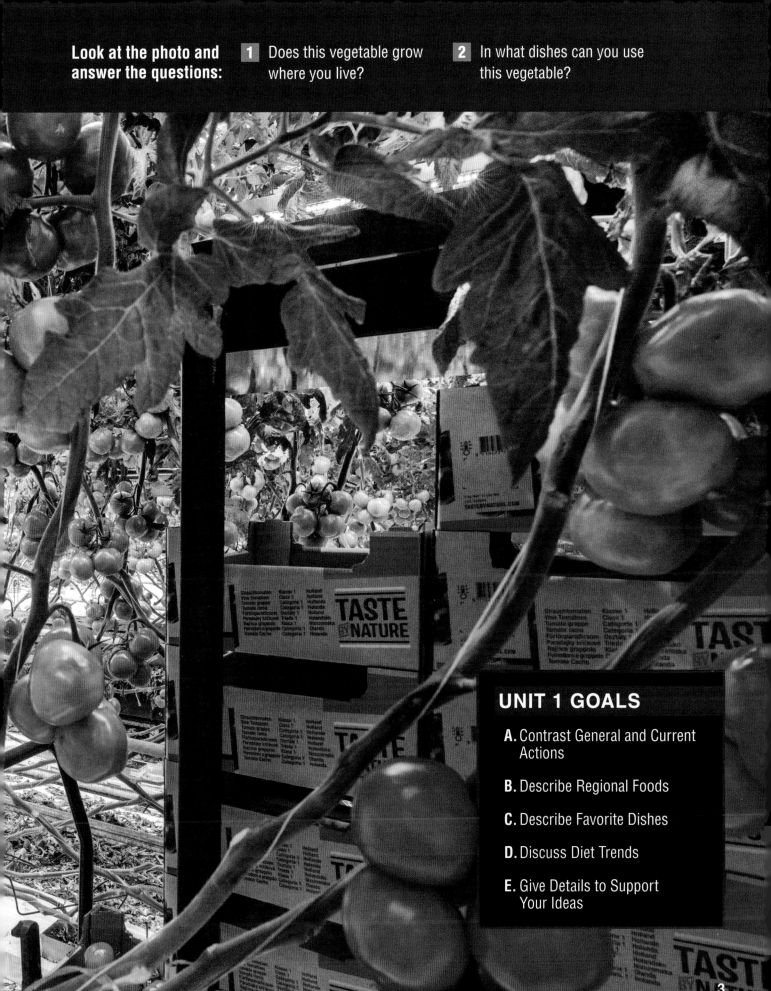

## UNIT 1 GOALS

**A.** Contrast General and Current Actions

**B.** Describe Regional Foods

**C.** Describe Favorite Dishes

**D.** Discuss Diet Trends

**E.** Give Details to Support Your Ideas

# GOAL Contrast General and Current Actions

### Vocabulary

**A** Read the suggestions for healthy eating.

**Vibrant farmers' market in Funchal, Madeira Island, Portugal**

## Tips for a Healthy Diet

Nowadays, many people are trying to eat a healthier diet. Eating healthy meals is not hard to do. Here are some easy ways to eat better:

- Take the time to prepare delicious dishes that are also good for you. Food you make at home is usually healthier than food from a restaurant or cafeteria.

- Eat dishes with healthy ingredients, such as vegetables, and ones without much sugar or salt.

- In many places, fresh food is available at farmers' markets. Farmers bring a variety of crops to these markets, including many kinds of fruits and vegetables.

- Although most of your meals should be healthy, it is fine to enjoy some ice cream or cookies on special occasions like your birthday.

**B** Write each word in blue next to the correct meaning.

1. _____ the kind of food you usually eat

2. _____ to make something ready

3. _____ better or more important than other things

4. _____ breakfast, lunch, and dinner

5. _____ describes something you can find or get

6. _____ plants grown by farmers for food

7. _____ food that is cooked in a certain way

8. _____ different kinds of something

9. _____ people who grow and produce food

10. _____ types of food that are combined to make a dish

## Grammar

| Simple Present and Present Continuous | |
|---|---|
| Use the simple present to talk about habits and things that are generally true. | I normally don't **eat** eggs for breakfast. <br> Fresh vegetables **are** always available at the market. |
| Use the present continuous to talk about actions and events that are happening now. | My father **is preparing** a special dish for tonight's dinner, and I **am watching** and **learning** how to make it. |
| To form questions, use **do/does** with the simple present and **am/are/is** with the present continuous. | **Do** you **follow** a special diet? <br> **Is** she **celebrating** her birthday tonight? |

**C** Discuss the statements below in pairs. Which things does the speaker usually do? Which things is the speaker doing right now?

**a.** I am eating an apple.

**b.** I eat breakfast at 9.

**c.** I buy fruit at the grocery store.

**d.** I am making coffee for you.

**D** Complete each sentence with the simple present or present continuous form of the verb.

1. My mother and I _____ (prepare) a meal together every afternoon.

2. In Mexico, most people _____ (eat) a big meal in the afternoon.

3. Right now, my mother and I _____ (make) a dish called *enchiladas*.

4. I really like enchiladas. Sometimes I _____ (have) them for breakfast!

5. Now my mother _____ (tell) the whole family to come to the table.

6. We _____ (enjoy) at least one meal together every day.

**E** In pairs, take turns doing the following.

1. Tell your partner what you usually eat for breakfast and lunch.

2. Tell your partner three things people you know are doing right now.

**F** Use the phrases in the box to talk about things...

...you usually do.

...you never or almost never do.

...you are doing (or not doing) right now.

> carry a cell phone
> check your email
> climb a mountain
> eat fruit for breakfast
> eat lunch in a cafeteria
> practice English grammar
> talk with a classmate
> try new foods
> wear athletic shoes

 **GOAL CHECK**
## Contrast General and Current Actions

Complete this sentence three times. Two of the sentences should be true, but one should be false: I usually _____, but today I'm _____.

Read your sentences to a partner in any order. Your partner will guess which sentence is false.

> I usually wear glasses, but today I'm wearing contact lenses.

> I usually carry my phone to class, but today I'm letting my sister use it.

# B GOAL Describe Regional Foods

## Listening

**A** Look at the picture. In pairs, discuss these questions.

1. What are important foods that everyone in your country eats?

2. Where in the world do farmers grow rice?

3. Why do they grow it there?

**B** 🎧 2 Listen to the interview. Circle the correct letter.

1. Who is the interviewer talking to?

   **a.** a restaurant owner    **b.** a rice farmer    **c.** a news reporter

2. What is happening in the rice paddy today? People are...

   **a.** planting rice plants.    **b.** planting seeds.    **c.** letting water into the paddy.

3. What kind of climate does rice need?

   **a.** hot and dry    **b.** warm and wet    **c.** cool and humid

**C** 🎧 2 Listen again and answer the questions.

**WORD FOCUS**

Farmers **raise** or **grow crops**.

1. Why doesn't the rice farmer plant seeds like other farmers?

   _____

2. How is the rainfall this year? _____

3. What happens to the water in the rice paddy after the rice plants grow?

   _____

4. What happens to the rice plants after they're dry? _____

# Communication

**D** Follow the instructions with a partner.

1. List some of the foods that grow well in your part of the world. They can be crops, meat, or seafood.

   _____      _____      _____

   _____      _____      _____

2. Talk about the dishes people make from each of these foods. What are the ingredients? Do you enjoy eating the dish?

**E** **MY WORLD** Do you try to buy local foods from farmers in your area? What are some advantages and disadvantages of doing this?

---

**PRONUNCIATION:** Linking Words Together

When a word ends in a consonant sound, and the next word begins with a vowel sound, the words are usually linked together.

| We cut the rice **plants and** clean them. | We **grow a lot of** rice. |

---

**F**  Listen to the sentences. Notice the pronunciation of the linked words. Then, listen again and repeat the sentences.

1. We're eating dinner now.
2. Her favorite dish is chicken with rice.
3. Famers work on weekends and holidays.
4. Paul and I don't like fish very much.
5. Coffee grows well in Colombia.
6. Rain falls in all seasons where I live.

---

✓ **GOAL CHECK** Describe Regional Foods

1. Think of a special dish from your area or region of the world. Take a few notes about each question below. Then use your notes to tell a partner about the special dish.

   What is the name of the dish?            When are the ingredients available?
   When do people usually eat it?           How do people prepare the dish?
   What are some of the ingredients?        How do you feel about the dish?

2. Get together with another pair and tell them about the special dishes you described.

> The dish is called *ceviche*, and it is popular in Peru. We make it with seafood and lime juice. Some of the other ingredients are...

## C GOAL Describe Favorite Dishes

### Language Expansion

**A** Look at the Healthy Eating Pyramid from Australia. In pairs, choose the correct phrase from the box to complete each sentence below.

| | |
|---|---|
| **a.** fish, beans, and nuts | **d.** milk, yogurt, and cheese |
| **b.** spinach, tomatoes, and carrots | **e.** pasta, bread, and rice |
| **c.** pineapples and grapes | **f.** pizza and canned foods |

1. Vegetables that are high in **vitamins** include _____.

2. Foods high in **protein** include meat, _____.

3. Many people eat **grains** at every meal. Grains include _____.

4. Many fruits are sweet. Fruits that have a lot of **sugar** in them include _____.

5. **Dairy** foods come from animals such as cows. _____ are all dairy.

6. Don't eat too much **salt**. Salty foods include _____.

### Grammar

**WORD FOCUS**

With the simple past, we often use:

yesterday / the day before yesterday

days / weeks / years / months **ago**

**last** week / month / year

| Simple Past | | |
|---|---|---|
| Use the simple past to talk about completed past actions or situations. | We **learned** how to make pizza yesterday. Our class **was** interesting last week. | |
| Some verbs are regular in the simple past. They have an -ed ending. | ask-asked<br>learn-learned | cook-cooked<br>need-needed |
| Some verbs are irregular in the simple past. | choose-chose<br>give-gave | eat-ate<br>go-went |

**B** Follow the instructions in pairs.

1. List 10 of your favorite things to eat and drink.

2. Talk about the nutrition in each item on your list. Use some of the **bold** words from **A**.

3. Plan a healthy meal. Explain your plan to another pair of students.

> Pasta is delicious. Do you think it's healthy?

> It has some protein and vitamins, but I don't think you should eat a lot of pasta.

> We chose peach yogurt as the dairy food. It has some sugar in it, but it's also high in protein.

**8** Unit 1

**C** Complete the conversation. Use the simple past of the verbs.

**Mary:** Tell me about yourself, Pedro.

**Pedro:** Well, I love to travel. Last year, I (1) _____ (travel) to Greece.

**Mary:** Wow! You (2) _____ (go) to Greece?

**Pedro:** Yes, and I (3) _____ (meet) my friend Vasilys and his family there. They (4) _____ (show) me around Athens and (5) _____ (introduce) me to many new foods. We (6) _____ (eat) a lot!

**Mary:** That sounds like fun.

**Pedro:** It was. I (7) _____ (eat) seafood and lamb, and I (8) _____ (try) a dish...

**D** Complete each sentence so it is true for you. Use the simple past and words from the box. Then, share your sentences with a partner.

1. (eat) Yesterday, I _____.
2. (like) When I was a child, I _____.
3. (prepare) Last week, I _____.
4. (buy) The last time I went to the grocery store, _____.
5. (order) The last time I went to a restaurant, _____.

| |
|---|
| dairy |
| dish |
| grain(s) |
| meal |
| protein |
| salt |
| special |
| sugar |
| vegetable(s) |
| vitamins |

## Conversation

**E** 🎧 4  Close your book and listen to the conversation. What is Albert eating? What is it made from?

**Albert:** You should try this! My aunt made it.

**Mary:** Mmmm... Delicious! What is it?

**Albert:** It's called *couscous*. It's made from wheat.

**Mary:** And what's this on top of the couscous?

**Albert:** Mostly vegetables and some kind of sauce.

**Mary:** How did your aunt learn to cook it?

**Albert:** Her great-uncle married a woman from North Africa. That's where couscous is from. They always ate it on special occasions.

**Mary:** What an interesting family history!

**Albert:** Yeah, and a great family recipe.

**F** Practice the conversation. Tell your partner about foods from other parts of the world.

✓ **GOAL CHECK** Describe Favorite Dishes

My whole family ate my grandmother's spaghetti. Do you think I should write that?

You want to share a photo of your favorite dish on a social media website. In pairs, discuss what you should include in the post:

Why did you eat the dish?     Who prepared the dish?     What ingredients were in the dish?

Who ate the dish?     How did the dish taste?     Your idea: _____

## D GOAL Discuss Diet Trends

### Reading

**A** In pairs, describe diets that you or someone you know have followed. Were they effective?

**B** Read the title and the first sentence of each paragraph. Which of these popular diets is / are mentioned in the article?

a. vegan diet
c. low-calorie diet
b. paleo diet
d. raw foods diet

**C** Read the article. Write examples of different foods in the correct columns.

| Foods people eat on a paleo diet | Foods people do NOT eat on a paleo diet |
|---|---|
|  |  |
|  |  |

**D** Read the question at the end of the first paragraph. Match each answer below with the correct person. There is one extra answer.

a. A person who is following a paleo diet
b. Dr. Peter Ungar

1. _____ Maybe, because there are many choices at the supermarket.

2. _____ No, because not eating certain kinds of food isn't healthy or natural.

3. _____ Yes, because not eating foods from farmers is more natural.

### ✓ GOAL CHECK

Create a one-day menu plan for a paleo diet. What might that person eat for breakfast, lunch, dinner, and snacks? Then, discuss the questions.

1. Would this diet work well for you? Why?

2. Does the paleo diet seem enjoyable? Practical? Healthy?

# The Paleo Diet: Natural and Healthy?

Modern supermarkets give us many choices. There are colorful fruits and vegetables, fresh fish and meat, many kinds of bread, eggs, yogurt, and cheese. But at the same time, people in the modern world are **experiencing** health problems, such as diabetes and heart disease. Could the food we eat be causing some of these problems?

One explanation for modern health problems is that they began when human beings became farmers about 12,000 years ago. Around that time, people started growing and eating crops, such as wheat and rice. Some people believe that returning to an earlier way of eating—a "paleo diet" that includes only meat, fish, and fruits and vegetables—might be a solution to our modern health problems.

A paleo diet is special because it doesn't include grains, dairy foods, or legumes, such as peanuts or beans. For many of us, it is not possible to prepare our favorite dishes without these ingredients. But people who follow a paleo diet only eat foods people ate before farming began. They believe this is a more natural and healthier way to eat.

For Dr. Peter Ungar, the **truth** is not so simple. In human history, people have eaten a wide variety of foods. Early human beings lived in different places with different climates, so many kinds of food were available to our **ancestors**—including some grains—even before farming began. Dr. Ungar says our **ability** to eat in many different ways and to be healthy whether we live in the Arctic or in the tropics is the important thing. One thing is certain, though: If you do decide to try a paleo diet, remember that your meals might actually have less variety than the meals of your early ancestors.

**experience**  have something happen to you
**truth**  facts, not things that are imagined or invented
**ancestors**  parents, grandparents, and other people who lived before you
**ability**  quality or skill that makes it possible for you to do something

## Communication

**A** Discuss the questions in a small group.

Many social events include food. What do you know about each social event below? Where does it take place, how many people are there, and what do they usually eat and drink?

| | | |
|---|---|---|
| a birthday party | a dinner party | a family dinner |
| lunch with coworkers | an outdoor picnic | a wedding dinner or feast |

> You can have a picnic at a park or at the beach. It's very informal, and you might eat sandwiches or salads and fruit.

**B** Describe a recent social event in your life. What happened? What did you eat?

## Writing

**C** Read the information in the box. Then discuss the questions below.

> **Main Idea**
>
> When you are reading, it is important to look for the writer's main ideas. These are the important points or claims the writer wants to make. For example:
>
> *For Peter Ungar, the truth is not so simple.*
>
> *One explanation for modern health problems is that they began when humans became farmers thousands of years ago.*
>
> **Supporting Details**
>
> After you read a main idea, it is helpful to look for details—information that helps you understand the main idea or believe the writer's claim. For example:
>
> *...in human history, people have eaten a wide variety of foods.*
>
> *Many kinds of food were available to our ancestors.*

**WORD FOCUS**

**claim** something that a person says is true

1. What main idea do the details in the box above support?

2. How do the details help you understand or believe that main idea?

Plant-based lasagna is a healthy vegetarian meal.

**D** Read the paragraph from an internet food blog. Notice the main idea (underlined) and the details that support the main idea.

There are many good dishes to serve at a dinner party, but <u>I recommend baked lasagna</u>. It is great for parties because it is a dish you can make in advance. For example, if you have time the night before the party, you can make the lasagna and put it in the refrigerator until the next day. In addition, everyone seems to like lasagna. If your guests eat meat, you can make a meat and cheese lasagna, but if your guests are **vegetarian**, a vegetable lasagna is just as delicious. A good tomato sauce, together with the pasta and other ingredients, is really all you need. Lasagna can even be **vegan** if you can find good vegan "cheese" at the store. Finally, it's a good party food because you don't need to prepare a lot of other dishes when you serve lasagna. A simple green salad and some Italian bread go well with lasagna. And maybe some dessert—after all, it is a party!

**vegetarian** a person who does not eat meat, fish, or chicken
**vegan** contains no animal foods, including milk, cheese, or eggs

REAL LANGUAGE

Quotation marks can tell us a word is being used in an unusual way. Vegan "cheese," for example, is not made from milk.

**E** Read the paragraph again and complete the outline below.

**Main Idea:** I recommend baked lasagna for a dinner party.
**Supporting Details:** 1. You can make lasagna in advance.

2. _____

3. _____

**F** In a small group, brainstorm ideas for these possible writing topics. What ideas do you have about each topic? What details might you include?

Write about a social event you attended recently.

Write about a bad meal that you had.

Write about people's eating habits in your country or culture.

**G** Choose ONE topic from the list above and write a paragraph in your notebook. Your paragraph should have a main idea near the beginning and three or four supporting details.

WRITING NOTE

You can use **because** to introduce reasons. Notice the two places the blog writer uses **because**.

 **GOAL CHECK**
## Give Details to Support Your Ideas

In pairs, discuss the topic you chose.

# WIDE AWAKE BAKERY

**A** What do you think daily life is like for *bakers*— people who bake bread for a living? Discuss your ideas with a partner.

**In Your Opinion: A Baker's Life**

1. Bakers start working very early in the morning.   T   F

2. Bakers have to do the same thing over and over again.   T   F

3. Bakers are creative and make a variety of different breads.   T   F

4. Bakers make a food that is very important in people's daily diets.   T   F

5. Bakers need to practice a lot to become good at their job.   T   F

6. Bakers do a boring job. It's not very exciting work.   T   F

**B** Read a quotation from the manager of the Wide Awake Bakery in Ithaca, New York, USA. In pairs, talk about the meaning of the quotation.

*I don't want to say that the bakery is an experiment. But, it's more like... it's more like saying, "Why not? Why not do it right?"*

— Stefan Senders

**C** Watch the video and take brief notes. What do you notice about...

1. ...the two people in the video (Stefan Senders and David McInnis)?

   _____

2. ...the bakery (where the bread is made)?

   _____

3. ...the bread dough (before it is baked)?

   _____

4. ...the bread oven?

   _____

5. ...the finished bread (after it is baked)?

   _____

**D** In pairs, practice using the expressions from the video.

1. Tell each other about a time when you were "climbing the walls." Why were you so bored?

2. Tell each other about a time when you tried something and "nailed it."

**E** In pairs, talk about the meaning of the quotation below. Is McInnis really talking about dancing?

*"You're learning a dance, and you're thinking about the steps all the time. ... And when you learn the dance, you just kind of do it—you don't have to think about it anymore."*

—David McInnis

**F** Tell your partner about something you have learned to do well. What are the "steps"? How did you learn to do them?

**REAL LANGUAGE**

A **sweet spot** is a time or place where everything happens perfectly.

*When you study for an exam, find the sweet spot between not enough and too much study.*

**Look at the photo and answer the questions:**

**1** How do these men know each other?

**2** What do you think they are talking about?

Marine biologist chats with local salmon fisherman in Scotland.

**UNIT 2 GOALS**

A. Talk about Yourself

B. Make Small Talk with New People

C. Start a Conversation

D. Discuss Endangered Languages

E. Give Examples

## GOAL Talk about Yourself

### Vocabulary

**A** Read.

Selfies are an important part of how we talk about ourselves now!

Every culture around the world has different customs and different ways of communicating. So when you learn a language, you learn more than words.

People use language to communicate many different things. Greetings, such as "Hello" or "How are you?," show that we are friendly or polite. We also use language to connect with each other. Using the right words can show our family members that we love them, for example. We might also become friends with people who we speak to every day. Another good way to connect with people is by talking about our personal experiences.

In some cultures, it is common to ask questions when you meet someone for the first time. You might ask a new neighbor, "Have you recently moved to this city?" This kind of conversation can increase feelings of trust between people. In other cultures, though, asking this kind of question could make people uncomfortable. Once you have learned the rules of a language, you can communicate more easily and avoid communication problems.

**B** Circle the correct word or phrase. You may use a dictionary to help you.

1. A **custom** is something that *few* / *most* people in a certain place or culture do.

2. The **way** we do something is *how* / *why* we do it.

3. When you **communicate** with someone, you share *money* / *information* with them.

4. A **polite** person has good manners and is not *rude* / *nice* to other people.

5. When you **connect** with other people, you feel *closer* / *not as close* to them.

6. After a long day at work or school, most people **become** *sad* / *tired*.

7. Your **experiences** are things that you do or that *return* / *happen* to you.

8. If something happens *often* / *rarely*, it is **common**.

9. If the amount of something **increases**, there is *more* / *less* of it.

10. Most people **avoid** things they *like* / *don't like*.

## Grammar

| The Present Perfect vs. The Simple Past | |
|---|---|
| Use the present perfect to talk about actions that:<br>1. began in the past and continue until the present.<br>2. happened at an indefinite past time and affect the present.<br>3. happened more than once in the past. | 1. They **have known** each other since the first grade.<br>2. Tim **has traveled** alone before, so he's not nervous about his trip to India.<br>3. Ken and Takako **have been** to Peru five times. |
| Use the simple past for completed actions or situations at a specific past time. | ~~They have become parents in 2017.~~<br>They became parents in 2017. |

**C** Complete each sentence with the present perfect or simple past form of the verb.

1. I think Lee will do well on the test. He _____ (study) a lot for it.

2. Elena _____ (take) the same test last year.

3. Sam _____ (travel) to Argentina four times. He loves it there!

4. Jason doesn't want to call his mother tonight. He _____ (call) her every night for the past week.

5. We _____ (learn) some Arabic greetings and polite phrases before our trip to Qatar last year.

**D** Complete the questions. Ask a partner. If the answer is "yes," ask, "When?"

Have you ever...

1. eaten _____ food?

2. seen a movie from _____ (country)?

3. gone to _____ ?

4. played _____ ?

5. talked to _____ ?

> Have you ever talked to a movie star?
>
> Yes, I have.

 **GOAL CHECK** Talk about Yourself

Use the questions to interview a partner. Then switch roles.

**Interview Questions**

1. What is a custom from your culture that you really like?

2. What are some things you have done just to be polite?

3. When you meet new people, do you avoid talking to them, or do you try to communicate with them? Explain.

4. Talk about some of your closest friends. How did you become friends with them?

5. What was your favorite way to spend time with the people in your family?

6. Talk about an important experience in your life. How has it affected you?

# B GOAL Make Small Talk with New People

## Listening

**A** 🎧 6 These people are meeting for the first time. Listen to their conversations. Where are the people?

**Conversation 1** The speakers are in _____.

    **a.** a hospital    **b.** a school    **c.** an airport

**Conversation 2** These people are in _____.

    **a.** a restaurant    **b.** an apartment building    **c.** an office building

**B** 🎧 6 Listen again. What do the people make small talk about?

**Conversation 1** They make small talk about _____.

    **a.** classes    **b.** weather    **c.** clothes

**Conversation 2** They make small talk about _____.

    **a.** sports    **b.** TV shows    **c.** the neighborhood

**WORD FOCUS**

**make small talk**
talk about things that aren't important

**C** In pairs, decide what the speakers will talk about next. Think of two more ideas for each conversation.

---

**PRONUNCIATION:** *Have* or *Has* vs. Contractions

In statements with the present perfect, *have* and *has* are sometimes pronounced completely, but in informal speaking, contractions may be used.

---

**D** 🎧 7 Listen and repeat.

| **Have** | **Contraction** | **Has** | **Contraction** |
| --- | --- | --- | --- |
| I have | I've | she has | she's |
| you have | you've | he has | he's |
| we have | we've | it has | it's |
| they have | they've | | |

**WORD FOCUS**

Remember that *has* is pronounced with a /z/ sound.
*She **has** already watched that movie, so she doesn't want to see it again.*

**E** 🎧 8 Listen and circle the sentences you hear.

1. **a.** I have never gone skiing.    **b.** I've never gone skiing.
2. **a.** He has been to Colombia three times.    **b.** He's been to Colombia three times.
3. **a.** Linda has taken a scuba diving class.    **b.** Linda's taken a scuba diving class.
4. **a.** They have already eaten breakfast.    **b.** They've already eaten breakfast.
5. **a.** We have had three tests this week.    **b.** We've had three tests this week.
6. **a.** Michael has found a new job.    **b.** Michael's found a new job.

# Communication

**F** Read.

> English speakers often make small talk when they meet someone new. In general, small talk should make people feel more comfortable—not less comfortable—so the topics should not be very personal. For example, "Which department do you work in?" is a good question at work, but "How much money do you make?" is too personal.

**G** Circle the topics that are good for small talk when you meet someone for the first time. Then add two more ideas. Compare your ideas in pairs.

family     money     religion     school     sports     work     _____     _____

**H** In pairs, read the situations. Choose a question to ask for each situation. Then, write and practice brief conversations based on the situations.

**Situation 1**   Min-Hee talks to Judy. It's Judy's first day at this job.

     **a.** Are you new in this city?    **b.** Are you making a good salary here?

**Situation 2**   Andrei is from Russia. He talks to Eduardo at the International Students' Club. It's Eduardo's first meeting.

     **a.** Where are you from?    **b.** Do you practice a religion?

**Situation 3**   Mark lives in apartment 104. He meets his new neighbor Lisa in the apartment building.

     **a.** Do you like living here?    **b.** Are you married?

**Situation 4**   Liz is making small talk with another student in her class.

     **a.** What was your grade on the test?    **b.** Did you think the test was difficult?

**I** With your partner, discuss the "incorrect" answers from **H**. Why do you think those questions might make someone feel uncomfortable? Do you think it's the same in every culture?

## ✓ GOAL CHECK
### Make Small Talk with New People

In pairs, write four good questions to ask when you meet someone new. Then join another pair and ask and answer your questions. Are all of the questions good for making small talk?

Small talk on a beach

# C GOAL Start a Conversation

## Language Expansion: Starting a Conversation

**A** Read the questions below. Think of different ways to answer them.

**ENGAGE!**

Are you shy or outgoing when you meet new people? Do you like to make small talk?

### Starting a Conversation

How do you like this weather? Are you enjoying this class?
Did you hear about _____? (something in the news, for example)
How long have you been waiting? (for the elevator, the bus, the meeting to begin, etc.)

**B** In pairs, choose one of these situations. Try to make small talk for as long as you can. Then change partners and situations and practice again.

| | |
|---|---|
| at a welcome party for new students | waiting in line in the office cafeteria |
| at the airport | walking in the park |

## Grammar

**Present Perfect Signal Words:** *Already*, *Yet*, *Ever*, and *Never*

| | | |
|---|---|---|
| *already* | Use *already* with questions and affirmative statements to clarify if something has happened in the past. | **Has** Roberta **already left**? <br> We **have already studied** this. |
| *(not) yet* | Use *yet / not yet* in questions and negative statements for emphasis. | **Have** you **done** the writing homework **yet**? <br> John **hasn't sent** the text message **yet**. |
| *(not) ever* <br> *never* | Use *ever / never (not ever)* in questions and negative statements to talk about something that has or has not happened at any time before now. | **Have** you **ever** met her? <br> We **have never** lost our house keys. <br> We **haven't ever** been bored in class. |

**Two people, on their way home, start a conversation in Milan, Italy.**

**C** Two classmates are talking. Fill in the blanks in the conversation.

**A:** Have you ever traveled to another country?

**B:** No, I have (1) _____ left this country, but I want to go to Colombia someday. Some of my cousins live there.

**A:** I see. Have (2) _____ already met your Colombian cousins?

**B:** Yes, I have (3) _____ them already. They came here last year.

**A:** That's nice. Are there any other countries you want to visit?

**B:** I want to visit Australia someday. (4) _____ you ever been there?

**A:** No, I haven't (5) _____ been there. Why do you want to go?

**B:** Well, I learned about Australian Rules football last year, but I (6) _____ not played the game yet. Maybe I can play it in Australia!

**D** Practice the conversation in **C** with a partner.

**E** **MY WORLD** In pairs, discuss the questions about traveling.

**1.** What are some places you have traveled to?

**2.** Where would you like to go that you haven't been yet?

## Conversation

**F** 🎧 9 Close your book and listen to the conversation. What do the speakers decide to do about the homework?

**Tom:** Excuse me. Are you in my history class?
**Rita:** Yes! I saw you in class yesterday. I'm Rita.
**Tom:** Hi, Rita. I'm Tom. Is this your first class with Mr. Olsen?
**Rita:** Yes, it is, but I've heard good things about him. What about you?
**Tom:** I've taken his classes before, and they've always been good.
**Rita:** That's great. Have you already done the homework for tomorrow?
**Tom:** No, not yet. How about you?
**Rita:** Not yet. Maybe we can call each other to talk about it.
**Tom:** That's a great idea! I'll give you my number.

**SPEAKING STRATEGY**

After you answer a question, say **What about you?** or **How about you?** to keep the conversation going.

## ✓ **GOAL CHECK** Start a Conversation

Move around the class. Walk up to five classmates and start a short conversation. Choose a topic and use *Have you ever ...?*

| classes | foods | movies | sports | travels | your idea _____ |
|---------|-------|--------|--------|---------|------------------|

Have you ever taken a class with Ms. Lee before?

Yes, I took an art class with her.

# D GOAL Discuss Endangered Languages

## Reading

**A** In pairs, discuss the questions.

1. How many languages are spoken in your country?

2. How many languages do you speak?

3. Do you think language and culture are related?

**B** Are these statements true or false? Answer before you read the article. Then read and check.

1. Most people in the world speak a "large" language with many speakers.

2. We will not lose any more languages in the future.

3. Few people are learning the Maori language.

4. Technology is a danger to languages.

**C** For each idea, circle the TWO correct examples from the article.

1. world languages with the largest number of speakers

   Hindi        Maori        Spanish

2. Tuvan words that show a connection with animals

   *ak byzaa*        *songgaar*        *ezenggileer*

3. technology that helps save endangered languages

   telephones        the internet        talking dictionaries

 **GOAL CHECK**

Discuss the questions in a small group. Then share your ideas with another group or with the class.

1. Why might it be important to speak one of the world's "large" languages? Make a list of 3–4 reasons.

2. Why are organizations trying to save endangered languages? Why are those languages important?

# Endangered Languages

There are around 7,099 languages in the world today. However, most people speak the largest languages: Chinese, Spanish, English, Hindi, Russian, Arabic, and others. So what about the smaller languages? According to the UNESCO Atlas of the World's Languages in Danger, around one third of the world's languages now have fewer than 1,000 speakers. We may soon lose those languages completely. In fact, 230 languages became "**extinct**" between 1950 and 2010.

Unfortunately, when we lose a language, we also lose culture and knowledge. That's because people in different places have different ways of living and thinking. One example of this is the Tuvan language of southern Siberia. Tuvan people depend on animals for food and other basic needs. Their language shows this close connection between people and animals. The Tuvan word *ezenggileer*, for example, means "to sing with the **rhythms** of riding a horse." And the word *ak byzaa* is "a white **calf** less than one year old."

In some places, people are working to save traditional languages. Many schools in New Zealand now teach the Maori language. This helps connect native New Zealanders to their Maori culture. And in the United Kingdom, Welsh is spoken by around 500,000 people in Wales. The Welsh government is working to increase that number to one million by 2050.

Technology could be another important way to save **endangered** languages. National Geographic's Enduring Voices project has created "Talking Dictionaries." These dictionaries are the recorded voices of people communicating with each other. All of them are fluent speakers of endangered languages. And because these dictionaries are available to anyone

on the internet, people now and in the future can learn some of the vocabulary, the greetings, and the grammar rules of past languages.

**extinct** a language is extinct when it has no living speakers.
**rhythm** a regular series of sounds or movements
**calf** a young cow
**endangered** in danger of soon becoming extinct

**K. David Harrison, co-director of the Enduring Voices project, works with Abamu Degio and Anthony Degio to record songs in Koro Aka, an endangered language from northern India.**

# E | GOAL Give Examples

## Communication

**A** Discuss the questions in pairs.

1. Look at the box. Which ways to learn a language have you experienced?

2. Which has been the most helpful to you?

| | |
|---|---|
| conversations with a speaker of the language | language textbooks |
| | lists of vocabulary words |
| electronic dictionaries | television or movies |
| explanations from a teacher | other _____ |

**B** Read the information.

| Technology for Language Learning | |
|---|---|
| **Video Chat**<br>You're probably already using video chat with your friends and family. You can also find people to practice a new language with. | **Online Videos**<br>Many kinds of videos are online. They combine language and pictures, and they can show us different cultures as well. |
| **Apps**<br>A few apps help language learners practice new vocabulary. Some have electronic flashcards with words, definitions, and example sentences. | **Game Apps**<br>Using some apps is similar to playing video games. You work your way from level to level, and you can earn points as you go. |
| **News Broadcasts**<br>It's common for news agencies such as the BBC to broadcast stories from around the world. You can watch or read them for free. | **Social Media**<br>Many people find interest groups and "like" them on social media. It's a way to connect and communicate with people like yourself. |

**C** Discuss the questions in pairs.

1. Which of the technologies have you used? How have you used them?

2. How might each kind of technology be helpful for language learning?

3. What kinds of technology might be the most and least helpful for you? Why?

## Writing

**WRITING SKILL: Giving Examples**

Giving examples is a good way to help your reader understand your ideas. Two common ways to introduce examples are *such as* and *for example*.

> *Study tools, **such as** flash cards, can be helpful for learning new vocabulary.*

> *It's also important to find ways to hear a new language. **For example**, online videos and music are good for listening practice.*

**D** Complete the sentences.

1. An app for video chats, such as _____, can be helpful for practicing a new language.

2. There are several good ways to learn new vocabulary. For example, I like to use _____.

3. It's important to read something in your new language every day. For example, _____.

4. Don't forget to talk with people who can help you, such as _____ _____.

**E** In your notebook, make a list of 3–4 things you do and don't recommend for language learning. Use your own ideas and examples.

| Do | Don't |
|---|---|
| • Do find fun ways to practice the language. For example, use an app that seems like a game. | • Don't spend all your time reading things such as news reports. You can listen to them as well. |

**F** Exchange your list with a partner and answer the questions.

1. Do you understand everything on your partner's list?

2. Can you suggest any other examples for your partner to use?

## ✓ GOAL CHECK Give Examples

In small groups, look at the box. Talk about good ways for these different kinds of people to learn a language. Use examples.

> I think children learn a lot from language teachers. For example, they might sing songs or practice saying new words in class.

> That's true, and older students like to use social media websites, such as Facebook and Twitter.

| | |
|---|---|
| employees at a company | people such as you |
| high school or university students | tourists planning to visit another country |
| older people with free time | young children |

Watching movies is a great way to practice English.

# VIDEO JOURNAL

## MARIE'S DICTIONARY

**A** Read. Then choose the correct word or phrase.

Marie Wilcox is the last **fluent** speaker of the Wukchumni language. It's the Native American language of a group of people from central California.

Marie learned Wukchumni from her grandparents, who did not speak English at home. In recent years, Marie decided to create a Wukchumni **dictionary**.

1. If you are **fluent** in a language, you speak it very *well / badly*.

2. California is in the *eastern / western* United States.

3. Marie Wilcox had *teachers / family members* who spoke the Wukchumni language.

4. A **dictionary** is a book with the *words / history* of a language.

**Lake Success is a reservoir and dam that provides water to nearby small towns at the eastern edge of the Central Valley in Tulare County, California.**

**B** What parts of learning English have been easy or difficult for you? Rank the skills from 1 (easiest) to 5 (most difficult).

---

**Learning a Language**

☐ Learning the definitions or meanings of words.

☐ Learning **sounds** and being able to understand the language.

☐ Learning pronunciation and being able to speak the language.

☐ Learning grammar rules and making correct sentences.

☐ Having **confidence** in your language ability.

---

**sounds** things that you hear
**confidence** feeling comfortable and sure about your abilities

**C** Watch the video and match the actions with the correct person or people.

**a.** Marie Wilcox

**b.** Jennifer Malone (Marie's daughter)

**c.** Donovan Treglown (Marie's grandson)

1. _____ says she spoke English as a child

2. _____ tells a story about animals and people

3. _____ uses a machine to record the sounds of Wukchumni

4. _____ help Marie with the dictionary

5. _____ types slowly on the computer keyboard

**D** Watch again and answer the questions in your notebook.

1. How would you describe Marie?

2. How is Marie's family helping her?

3. Who speaks Wukchumni better, Marie's daughter or her grandson?

4. In the story, which animal won the race to the top of the mountain?

**E** Discuss the questions in groups.

1. What languages are spoken in your country? Do these languages have small or large numbers of speakers?

2. Do a lot of people in your country want to learn English or other widely spoken languages? Why?

3. What effects have English or other languages had on your country? For example, do most children still speak the same language as their grandparents?

Amsterdam-based architects won an international competition to design a pedestrian bridge over Dragon King Harbor River in Changsha, China.

**Look at the photo and answer the questions:**

**1** Is it important that cities be beautiful?

**2** Does your city have landmarks like bridges and rivers?

## UNIT 3 GOALS

**A.** Make Predictions about Your City or Town

**B.** Explain What Makes a Good Neighborhood

**C.** Discuss the Pros and Cons of City Life

**D.** Evaluate Solutions to a Problem

**E.** Explain What Makes a Good City

### Vocabulary

A Read the article.

**Manhattan's High Line Park**

## Changing Cities

By the year 2050, 66% of the people on Earth will live in large cities. That's around two-thirds of the world's population. Most of these people will live in tall apartment buildings, so it makes sense to design those buildings in ways that are good for the environment. Gardens on top of buildings, for example, save energy for heating and cooling. They are also a comfortable place for people to spend time—away from the traffic on the noisy city streets below.

Walking from place to place is a big part of city life. However, when pedestrians need to walk across streets, there can be problems. One solution to these problems are the "X-crossings" found in Tokyo, Japan and other cities. There, when the light turns red, all of the cars, buses, and other vehicles must stop. Then, the pedestrians can cross in any direction. Another solution could be neighborhoods with more shops and restaurants on every block. This makes it easier for people to walk to the places they need to go.

Every big city needs good ways for people to get around. In the future, more cities will have as many kinds of public transportation as Hong Kong. With more than seven million people in a fairly small area, Hong Kong is a crowded place. So, in addition to cars and taxis, Hong Kong residents ride buses, trains, boats, and streetcars—all good ways to get around the city.

B Write each word in blue next to the correct meaning.

1. _____ all of the people who live in a certain area

2. _____ parts of a city where people live

3. _____ machines, such as cars or trucks, that carry people or things from place to place

4. _____ people who are walking

5. _____ full of loud sounds

6. _____ all the vehicles moving on the roads in an area

7. _____ full of people

8. _____ plan how something should be

9. _____ all the ways of taking people or things from one place to another

10. _____ the number 1,000,000

**WORD FOCUS**

**traffic jam** so many vehicles in the street that they can't move

**population growth** a growing number of people living in a place

## Grammar

| Statements | The city **will be** safer for pedestrians. | Use *will* + the base form of a verb to talk about the future. |
|---|---|---|
| Negatives | We **won't have** space for any more traffic. | In speaking, we often use contractions with *will*: I'll, you'll, we'll, they'll, she'll, he'll. Note the irregular negative contraction for *will not: won't.* |
| *Yes / No* questions | **Will** the population **continue** to grow? | |
| *Wh-* questions | Where **will** people **live**? | |

**C** What do you think? Circle **Y** for *yes* or **N** for *no.* Compare answers in pairs.

In the year 2040...

1. My city will have a larger population than it does now.   Y   N
2. People will still drive cars in the city.   Y   N
3. Buildings will be taller than they are now.   Y   N
4. There will be more parks and gardens in the city.   Y   N

**D** Complete the sentences with words from the box.

1. Adam will _____ in Vancouver, Canada all next week.
2. That's great! _____ he take a tour of Vancouver?
3. Yes, that way he will _____ different neighborhoods.
4. Will _____ use the public transportation there?
5. I think so. He probably won't _____ to spend money on taxis.
6. That sounds great. I think he will really _____ his visit!

| be |
|---|
| enjoy |
| he |
| see |
| want |
| will |

**E** In pairs, think about the city or town you are in now. What will it be like 10 years from now?

| enough jobs for everyone | a larger population |
|---|---|
| many shops and restaurants | more vehicles and traffic jams |
| safer ways for pedestrians to cross streets | several kinds of public transportation |
| taller apartment buildings | your idea _____ |

| Our city will have... | Our city won't have... |
|---|---|
| | |

> Will our city have a larger population 10 years from now?

> I think so. People will move here from the countryside.

 **GOAL CHECK**

## Make Predictions about Your City or Town

Join another pair of students and talk about the future of your city or town. Use your list from **E** and *will* or *won't.*

> In 10 years, our city will have a larger population.

> Yes, but there won't be enough jobs for all of those people.

# GOAL  Explain What Makes a Good Neighborhood

## Listening

**A** Discuss these questions in pairs.

1. How often do you go to a park?

2. What do you do there?

3. What do you think about the parks in your city or town?

**B** 🎧 11  Listen to a radio program about a park in Paris called the Jardin Nomade. Circle the correct letter.

1. The Jardin Nomade is unusual because it's so _____.

   **a.** old              **b.** large          **c.** small

2. In the Jardin Nomade, people _____.

   **a.** grow food        **b.** play sports    **c.** enjoy art

3. Isabel Dupont and her neighbors will help other neighborhoods _____.

   **a.** next week        **b.** next month     **c.** next year

**C** 🎧 11  Listen again. Answer each question in your notebook.

1. What year did the park start?

2. How many gardens do people have in the park?

3. What do the neighbors eat there every month?

4. How many people come to the monthly dinners?

5. How many parks like this are there in Paris now?

**D** **MY WORLD** What are some of the special things in your city? Answer the question in pairs.

---

**PRONUNCIATION:** Stressed Syllables Before -tion Suffix

The syllable before the suffix -tion is stressed. This means the sound is a little longer and louder than other syllables in the word.

---

**E** 🎧 12  Listen and repeat. Put the stress on the syllable in **bold**.

1. popu**la**tion                    4. pol**lu**tion

2. transpor**ta**tion                5. e**mo**tion

3. pronunci**a**tion                 6. at**ten**tion

**F** In pairs, make new sentences using the words in **E**.

> The population of the city will probably grow.

## Conversation

**G** 🎧 13 Close your book and listen to the conversation.

**Ben:** How do you like living in your neighborhood?

**Sarah:** Well, it has a lot of beautiful old buildings, but there are some problems.

**Ben:** Like what?

**Sarah:** It doesn't have many different stores. There's only one supermarket, so food is very expensive.

**Ben:** That sounds like a pretty big problem.

**Sarah:** It is, but the city is building a new shopping center now. Next year, we'll have more stores.

**H** Practice the conversation in pairs. Then discuss the questions.

1. What is good about the neighborhood? What is bad?

2. How will the neighborhood be different in the future?

**I** Write the words or phrases from the box in the correct column in your notebook. Add two more ideas to each column.

**Back Bay neighborhood in Boston, US**

| Good things in a neighborhood | Bad things in a neighborhood |
|---|---|
| | |

beautiful buildings
crime
heavy traffic
a lot of noise
pollution
public transportation
shops and restaurants
trees and green space

**J** In pairs, make a conversation. Use your ideas from **I**.

**K** What are the three most important things for a good neighborhood? Talk in pairs about your ideas in **I**. Make a new list together. Give reasons.

| Most important things for a good neighborhood | Reason |
|---|---|
| 1. | |
| 2. | |
| 3. | |

 **GOAL CHECK**
## Explain What Makes a Good Neighborhood

Explain your list to the class.

**GOAL** Discuss the Pros and Cons of City Life

**Language Expansion:** City Life

art museums
buses and trains
coffee shops
concert halls
government buildings
movie theaters
parks and gardens
shopping centers
sports arenas

**A** Look at the list. Discuss the questions in pairs.

**1.** Which places might you visit for entertainment?

**2.** Which places might you visit for relaxation?

**3.** Which places might you visit for some other purpose?

**B** **MY WORLD** What public places do you visit in your city or town? Are there any places on the list where you have never been?

## Grammar

| Will + Time Clauses | |
|---|---|
| A time clause says when something happens. We often use *before* or *after* at the beginning of a time clause. | I will look at the neighborhood carefully **before I choose a new apartment.** **After I move into my new apartment,** I'll meet my neighbors. |
| In a sentence about the future, use the simple present in the time clause. | They will design the garden **after they talk** to all of the neighbors. |
| The time clause can come first or second in the sentence. If the time clause comes first, it is followed by a comma. | **Before I choose a new apartment,** I will look at the neighborhood carefully. |

**Light shining on the busy city of Bogotá, Colombia.**

**C** Ask and answer the questions in pairs. Use time clauses and the family's plan for their city vacation.

1. What will they do after they arrive?

> After they arrive, they will take a taxi to their hotel and check in.

2. What will they do after they check in at the hotel?

3. What will they do before they visit the art museum?

4. What will they do after they visit the art museum?

5. What will they do before they leave Bogotá?

- **Monday:** Arrive in Bogotá, Colombia at 1:15 p.m.
- Take a taxi to hotel; check in at the hotel.
- Walk to the Plaza Bolívar; take pictures.
- Visit the Botero museum.
- Eat dinner at a restaurant.
- **Tuesday:** Take a tour of the city.

## Conversation

**D** 🎧 14 Close your book and listen to the conversation. Where does each speaker live?

**Sofía:** What a great day it's been!

**Hana:** I agree! When will you come downtown to visit me again?

**Sofía:** Maybe I'll come next Saturday. I want to see the new shopping center.

**Hana:** That sounds good, but I have my yoga-in-the-park class on Saturday mornings.

**Sofía:** Will you be free after you finish class?

**Hana:** Yes. We could have lunch before we go to the shopping center.

**Sofía:** Great! It sounds like another perfect day in the city.

**Hana:** And maybe I can visit you in the suburbs soon.

**E** Read about Sofía's situation.

> Sofía likes living in a suburb outside the city. It is quiet and there are many green spaces, such as parks and gardens. On the other hand, Sofía enjoys visiting her friend in the city. She is thinking about moving downtown, but she has not yet made up her mind.

**F** Think of reasons why Sofía should or shouldn't move downtown. Finish her list of pros and cons.

| Pros—Good things about city life | Cons—Bad things about city life |
|---|---|
| 1. Easy to visit interesting museums | 1. City apartments are more expensive |
| 2. | 2. |
| 3. | 3. |
| 4. | 4. |

## GOAL CHECK
## Discuss the Pros and Cons of City Life

Share your lists of pros and cons with a small group. Discuss what you think Sofía will do.

> Do you think Sofía will move downtown?

> Maybe, but she won't like the noise.

## D GOAL Evaluate Solutions to a Problem

### Reading

**A** Look at the topics in the box. In pairs, talk about how easy it is to do these things in your city.

> eating out      finding a park      going to school
> walking in your neighborhood

**B** Scan the reading to find the information.

1. The name of a person _____

2. The title of a book _____

3. The names of three cities _____

**C** Read the article. Circle the correct option.

1. Walking in cities can be *slow* / *dangerous*.

2. Engwicht wants cities to be better for *pedestrians* / *vehicles*.

3. Nowadays, people have *more* / *less* contact with their neighbors.

4. *Brisbane* / *Boston* is working to make its streets safer.

5. Engwicht travels all over *Australia* / *the world* with his message.

### Communication

**D** Discuss the questions in pairs.

1. How much walking do you usually do?

2. Where do you usually walk?

3. Do you feel safe when you are walking? Explain.

### ✓ GOAL CHECK

Your city wants to improve pedestrian safety. Rank the safety measures from 1 (most helpful) to 5 (least helpful). Then, in pairs, compare and discuss your answers.

_____ more or better crosswalks

_____ lower speed limits

_____ fewer cars in the city

_____ more or better sidewalks

_____ (your idea)

# Streets for People

Walking is a great way to get around. For short trips, for exercise, or just for fun, walking can be better than driving or riding. But in many cities, walking can also be dangerous. Cars, trucks, and motorcycles are a danger to pedestrians, and sometimes there are **accidents**.

David Engwicht, from Brisbane, Australia, wants to do something about this. His book, *Reclaiming Our Cities and Towns*, has a simple message: We need to take back our streets and make them better places for walking.

In the past, Engwicht says, streets belonged to everybody. Children played there, and people walked to work or to stores. Now, however, most city engineers design streets for vehicles, such as cars, trucks, and buses. People stay inside buildings to get away from the crowded **sidewalks**, the noisy streets, and the dangerous traffic. Unfortunately, this gives them less contact with their neighbors.

Many cities are working to make their streets safer for pedestrians. There are new **crosswalks** on the streets and more traffic lights and bicycle **lanes**. The city of Florence, Italy, only allows cars and buses with special **permits** to drive on its historic city streets. In Boston, US, the Slow Streets program gives some neighborhoods more stop signs and a 20 mph (32 kph) speed limit. These cities hope there will be fewer accidents in the future.

Engwicht travels around the world, helping people think differently about pedestrians, streets, and neighborhoods. Whether we live in a small town or a city with a population in the millions, Engwicht says we should think of streets as our "outdoor living room." Changing the traffic is just the beginning. In the future, streets may again be safe places for people, and walking will be an even better form of transportation than it is now.

**accident** something harmful or unpleasant that happens by surprise
**sidewalk** a path with a hard surface along the side of a street
**crosswalk** a place where drivers must stop to let pedestrians cross a street
**lane** a part of a street that is marked with painted lines
**permits** official documents that allows you to do something

# GOAL Explain What Makes a Good City

## Communication

**A** Look at the chart. Discuss the questions below in pairs.

| City A | City B |
|---|---|
| • good weather, sunny days<br>• plenty of jobs<br>• safe<br>• art, music, culture | • good schools, education<br>• parks, outdoor spaces<br>• public transportation<br>• safe for pedestrians |

1. How does each item in the chart improve city life?

2. Which city would you rather live in? Why?

> People spend time outdoors on sunny days.

> And they might get more exercise.

**B** **MY WORLD** Answer the question in pairs.

Think about your hometown or the city where you are now. Which of the items from the chart in **A** does your city have?

## Writing

**WRITING SKILL: Topic Sentences**

Most paragraphs in English begin with a topic sentence. The topic sentence tells us:

1. the main idea (What is the paragraph about?)
2. the controlling idea (What does the paragraph say about the topic?)

A good topic sentence helps the reader understand your ideas.

**WRITING NOTE**

The words **also** and **and** can show that you are moving on to the next idea.

**C** Read the paragraph.

main idea        controlling idea
Green spaces increase the quality of life in cities. Parks, beaches, and other green spaces are good places to be active. Playing sports and doing other kinds of recreation helps people in cities stay healthy. These spaces **also** give people contact with nature. Seeing green plants and hearing birds in the trees are pleasant breaks from a noisy city. **And** because they are good places for special events, green spaces can make communities stronger. Hearing a concert in the park with friends and neighbors, for example, is a great way to enjoy city life.

**D** Discuss the questions in pairs.

1. Where is the topic sentence located?

2. What are the three ways green spaces increase quality of life?

3. What other details does the writer include?

**People rowing boats and cycling in Central Park, New York**

**E** Choose the best topic sentence for the paragraph below.

**a.** My city has numerous good places to work.

**b.** The national university is located in my city.

**c.** Good schools are one of the best things about my city.

_____. For children, there are excellent public schools and private schools. Parents can decide which kind of school is best for their child. For older students, the national university is located in my city. It is quite large, and it attracts top professors from here and around the world. And for people who want job training, my city has several technical schools. They offer programs in everything from nursing to solar-energy technology. All of these education options help to make my city a good place to live.

**F** In your notebook, write a paragraph with a good topic sentence.

**1.** Choose one of the items from the chart in **A**.

**2.** Explain how or why it makes city life better.

✓ **GOAL CHECK** Explain What Makes a Good City

In pairs, share your ideas about how or why these things make city life better.

# VIDEO JOURNAL

# TEDTALKS

# HOW TO REINVENT THE APARTMENT BUILDING

**A** In pairs, talk about architecture in your city. Does your city have high-rise buildings? Does your city have creative buildings or traditional ones?

**B** Discuss the questions with a partner.

1. What are some of the high-density cities in the world?

2. What interesting buildings do you know about?

3. Do you think most high-rise apartment buildings are beautiful? Nice to live in? Why?

**Habitat 67 is a housing complex in Montreal, Canada designed by architect Moshe Safdie.**

**C** Watch the video. Number the places in the order you see and hear about them.

___ Beijing, China

___ Philadelphia, US

___ Singapore

___ Hong Kong, China

___ São Paulo, Brazil

**D** Complete each sentence from the video with a word or phrase.

1. Let's design a building which gives the qualities of a _____ to each unit.

2. In 1973, I made my first trip to _____.

3. This is Beijing then—not a single _____ building in Beijing or Shanghai.

4. So a few years ago, we decided to _____ and rethink Habitat.

5. And we realized it's basically about light, it's about _____, it's about nature.

**E** Work in pairs.

1. At the end of the video, you see Safdie's building called Marina Bay Sands in Singapore. List several things you and your partner might like and dislike about living there.

| Things we might like | Things we might dislike |
|---|---|
|  |  |

2. Do you think buildings like Safdie's will become more popular in the future? Why?

MOSHE SAFDIE
Architect

Moshe Safdie's **idea worth spreading** is that apartment buildings should be habitats that provide light, nature, and user-friendly spaces for their inhabitants. Watch Safdie's full TED Talk on TED.com.

Crystal Thornburg-Homcy
surfing in Big Sur, California

**Look at the photo and answer the questions:**

**1** What words could you use to describe the photo?

**2** How does this kind of activity keep people healthy?

## UNIT 4 GOALS

A. Discuss Ways to Stay Healthy

B. Talk about Healthy Lifestyles

C. Suggest Helpful Natural Remedies

D. Describe the Benefits of a Positive Attitude

E. Explain an Idea Using Details

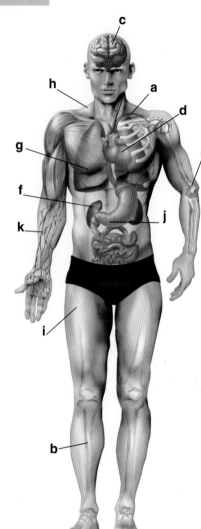

# A | **GOAL** Discuss Ways to Stay Healthy

## Vocabulary

**A** Look at the picture. Fill in the blanks with the vocabulary words from the box.

| a. artery | b. bone | c. brain | d. heart | e. joint | f. ~~kidney~~ |
|-----------|---------|----------|----------|----------|------------|
| g. lungs | h. muscle | i. skin | j. stomach | k. vein | |

1. This pushes your blood through your body: _____

2. These carry blood around your body: _____ , _____

3. These bring air into your body: _____

4. This covers the outside of your body: _____

5. These make your body move: _____ , _____

6. This lets you think and remember: _____

7. This is one of the organs that cleans your blood: ____*kidney*____

8. This digests food: _____

9. This supports your body: _____

**B** 🎧 16 Listen and check (✓) the words you hear.

| ☐ artery | ☐ bone | ☐ brain | ☐ heart | ☐ joint | ☐ kidney |
|----------|--------|---------|---------|---------|----------|
| ☐ knee | ☐ lungs | ☐ muscle | ☐ skin | ☐ stomach | ☐ vein |

## Grammar

### The Comparative, Superlative, and Equative

| The **comparative** expresses similarities or differences between two people or things.<br><br>Form the comparative with an adjective + *-er* + *than* or *more* / *less* + adjective + *than*. | Henry is **healthier than** his father.<br><br>A cold is **less serious than** the flu.<br><br>Nothing is **more important than** good health. |
|---|---|
| The **superlative** expresses extremes among three or more people or things.<br><br>Form the superlative with *the* + adjective + *-est* or *the most* / *least* + adjective. | Walking is **the healthiest** exercise for many older adults.<br><br>Having good social connections is **the most beneficial** thing we can do for our health. |
| The **equative** is used when two people or things are or are not the same, use this pattern: *(not) as* + adjective + *as* | Sitting for too long can be **as harmful as** smoking cigarettes.<br><br>For me, swimming in a pool is **not as enjoyable as** taking a yoga class. |

Add *-er* / *-est* to most adjectives with 1 or 2 syllables.

Use *more* / *less* or *the most* / *least* with some 2-syllable adjectives and all adjectives of 3 or more syllables.

When adjectives end in *-y*, change the *-y* to *-i* and add *-er* / *-est*.

Some adjectives have irregular comparative and superlative forms:

good / better / best

bad / worse / worst

far / farther / farthest

C Complete the sentences. Use the comparative, superlative, or equative forms, and the words in parentheses.

1. Walking for exercise is _____ (good) than running.

2. Some elderly people are _____ (healthy) as some young people.

3. Too much stress is _____ (bad) thing for your body.

4. Getting enough sleep is _____ (beneficial) as getting enough exercise.

5. Playing tennis is _____ (not, enjoyable) as playing basketball.

6. Eating healthy food is _____ (less important) than drinking plenty of water.

D Do you agree or disagree with the statements above? Discuss in pairs, using the comparative, superlative, and equative forms.

> I agree. Walking is easier on the knees.

> Yes, but running gives me a better workout.

## Communication

E In pairs, complete the table with ideas from the box. Add your own ideas.

contact with friends & family
playing sports
sleeping 7–8 hours

eating fruits & vegetables
reading a good book
taking a walk

| Ways to Stay Healthy | | |
|---|---|---|
| Daily Life | Exercise Routine | Other |
|  |  |  |

F Discuss the table in E. Which things are more important or less important for staying healthy?

✓ **GOAL CHECK** Discuss Ways to Stay Healthy

In pairs, talk about things you do to stay healthy. Complete these sentences:

I try to _____.

I try not to _____.

> I try to walk as much as possible.

> I try not to eat a lot of sugar.

# B GOAL Talk about Healthy Lifestyles

## Listening

**A** Discuss the questions in pairs.

1. What determines how healthy you are?

2. Are your **genes** or your **lifestyle** more important?

**B** 🎧 17 Listen to three people talk about their health. Write the letter (A–C) to match the speaker to the correct topic.

1. Exercise _____    2. Diet _____    3. Healthy genes _____

**C** 🎧 17 Listen again and answer the questions in your notebook.

**Speaker A:**

1. What kind of exercise does Speaker A get?

2. Which family members does Speaker A mention?

**Speaker B:**

3. What kind of exercise does Speaker B get?

4. How often does Speaker B get sick?

**Speaker C:**

5. Why did Speaker C change her diet when she got older?

6. What do some people think about Speaker C's diet?

Working in a community garden can be a good form of exercise.

**D** **MY WORLD** Interview a partner. Then tell the class about your partner's lifestyle.

- Exercise: What kind do you get? How often?
- Diet: What do you usually eat?

---

**PRONUNCIATION:** Linking with the Comparative and Superlative

When we use the comparative -er or more, and the next word starts with an /r/ sound, the words are linked together.

When we use the superlative -est or most, and the next word starts with a /t/ sound, the words are linked together.

   She'll run in a **longer race** next month.    We had the **best time** of our lives.

---

**E** 🎧 18   Listen to the sentences. Notice how the sounds are linked. Listen again and repeat.

1. Watching a sunset is more relaxing than watching TV.
2. This is the best tea for your stomach.
3. My grandfather is a faster runner than I am.
4. Which exercise is the most tiring?
5. You'll need a better reason than that.
6. I like to buy the freshest tomatoes I can find for my salads.

## Communication

**F** What are the best kinds of food and exercise for a healthy lifestyle? In pairs, rate the foods from least healthy (1) to healthiest (5). Add one idea of your own. Then do the same with the types of exercise. Compare your list with the list of another pair.

> I feel good if I eat some meat or fish every day.

____ bread  ____ fruit  ____ meat  ____ vegetables  ____ _____

> But is meat healthier than vegetables?

____ running  ____ swimming  ____ walking  ____ yoga  ____ _____

---

✓ **GOAL CHECK** Talk about Healthy Lifestyles

> Our generation is healthier because doctors know more now than in the past.

Discuss the questions in a small group. Use some of the ideas below and your own ideas.

Is your generation (the people near your age) healthier or less healthy than your parents' or your grandparents' generation? Why do you think so?

> Are our parents healthier because they spend more time with friends and neighbors?

| | |
|---|---|
| a healthy diet | contact with friends and family |
| doctors and medicine | enough exercise |
| having energy to do things | living a long time |
| your idea: _____ | your idea: _____ |

# GOAL  Suggest Helpful Natural Remedies

## Language Expansion: Everyday Ailments

For every common health problem, there's a product for sale to cure it. Are you suffering from insomnia? There's a pill to help you fall asleep. Did a pimple appear on your face? There's a cream for that. If you have a headache after a long day at work, or perhaps a sore throat and fever, you can buy something to make you feel better. Do you have indigestion because you ate the wrong kind of food? There's a pill to end the burning feeling in your stomach. If food won't stay in your stomach at all, you can take some medicine to end the nausea. Or maybe you ate too fast, so now you have the hiccups. Well, you won't find anything at the pharmacy for hiccups, but there's probably a company working on a new product for that right now.

**A** Write the words in blue next to their definition.

1. _____ not being able to sleep

2. _____ high body temperature

3. _____ a repeated sound in your throat, often from eating too quickly

4. _____ a feeling that what's in your stomach will come up

5. _____ pain in the stomach because of something you have eaten

6. _____ a small raised spot on the skin

7. _____ a pain in your head

8. _____ a general feeling of pain in the throat

> I know about using olive oil to help with dry skin.

**B** Read the article about natural remedies. What other natural remedies do you know about?

> Interesting! Have you tried it?

## A Natural Solution

Garlic for a cold? Mint for bad breath? These days, more and more people are turning to their grandparents' remedies to cure their minor illnesses. And why not? These natural remedies are usually safe, inexpensive, and best of all—they work! (At least for some of the people, some of the time.) So the next time you're looking for a cure, skip the pharmacy and head to the grocery store for:

- **lemons** to stop the hiccups (Bite into a thick slice.)
- **ginger** to end nausea (Grind it and add hot water to make a tea.)
- **milk** to cure insomnia (Drink a warm glass at bedtime.)
- **honey** to help a sore throat (Mix it with warm water and drink it slowly.)
- **onions** to relieve a headache (Put slices on your forehead, close your eyes, and relax.)

## Grammar

| Infinitive of Purpose | |
|---|---|
| The infinitive of purpose gives a reason for doing something. Form an infinitive with *to* + the base form of a verb. | You can drink tea with honey **to help** a sore throat. I use sunscreen **to protect** my skin. |
| *In order to* + the base form of a verb is another way to express the infinitive of purpose. | Nikki took an aspirin **in order to lower** her fever. |
| Use a comma after the infinitive of purpose when it begins a sentence. | **To stop hiccups,** I drink a glass of water. |

C Match the actions with the reasons.

1. Get plenty of sleep at night _____
2. Eat fruits and vegetables _____
3. Take a nap _____
4. Give children warm milk _____
5. Ask your doctor questions _____
6. Lift weights _____

a. to help them fall asleep.
b. to find out the best remedy for your problem.
c. to feel rested during the day.
d. to make your muscles stronger.
e. to get enough vitamins in your diet.
f. to cure a headache.

## Conversation

D 🎧 19 Close your book and listen to the conversation. What remedies for fatigue do the speakers talk about?

**REAL LANGUAGE**

We say **'That's new'** when we notice something different or unusual.

**Olivia:** Hi, Ashley. Are you drinking coffee? That's new.

**Ashley:** Hi, Olivia. You're right. I usually don't drink coffee, but I need it today to wake up.

**Olivia:** You do look tired. Did you get enough sleep last night?

**Ashley:** No, I was worried about today's test, so it was hard to fall asleep.

**Olivia:** Come on. Let's go for a walk.

**Ashley:** Go for a walk? Why?

**Olivia:** To wake you up and to get some oxygen to your brain before the test.

**Ashley:** That's a good idea. Where do you want to go?

E Practice the conversation in pairs. Find and underline the infinitives of purpose.

F **MY WORLD** In pairs, discuss which ailments from **A** you or your friends sometimes have. Do you think they are serious health problems?

---

✔ **GOAL CHECK** Suggest Helpful Natural Remedies

Join another pair. Follow the steps.

1. Tell the other pair which ailments from **A** you talked about.
2. Ask them to suggest remedies for those ailments. Then switch roles.

We sometimes have insomnia.

You could read for a while to relax.

# D  GOAL  Describe the Benefits of a Positive Attitude

## Reading

**A** Tell a partner what makes you feel a lot of stress.

| | | |
|---|---|---|
| going to the doctor or dentist | meeting new people | speaking to a group |
| taking an important exam | traveling by car, plane, etc. | your idea: _____ |

**B** Do you think stress is harmful to your health? Explain your answer to your partner.

**C** Read the text. Match each university to the correct research result.

| | |
|---|---|
| **1.** ___ University of Wisconsin | **a.** Helping other people can keep you healthy when you are under stress. |
| **2.** ___ Harvard University | **b.** People who believe stress prepares them for a challenge have open, relaxed blood vessels under stress. |
| **3.** ___ University at Buffalo | **c.** The belief that stress is harmful to one's health can be harmful to one's health. |

**D** Circle **T** for *true* or **F** for *false*. Then correct the false statements to make them true.

1. For the University of Wisconsin study, participants were asked two questions.  **T**  **F**

2. The way you think about stress affects how your body reacts to stress.  **T**  **F**

3. Stress always causes blood vessels to become narrower.  **T**  **F**

4. People who had a lot of contact with others had a higher risk of dying.  **T**  **F**

**E** Complete the list of dos and don'ts with information from the article.

1. Don't believe that _____.

2. Do believe that signs of stress _____.

3. Do spend a lot of time _____.

## ✓ GOAL CHECK

Form a small group with 2–3 other students. Discuss the questions.

1. What do you remember about the three research studies?

2. In each study, why were the participants' attitudes important?

3. Talk about a time when a positive attitude helped you in some way.

# Attitude Is **Everything**

Kelly McGonigal is a health psychologist with some good news: **Stress** may not be the **enemy** of good health. McGonigal came to this conclusion after looking at three important health studies. In the first study, researchers at the University of Wisconsin asked 30,000 adults how much stress they had experienced during the past year. They also asked whether the **participants** thought this stress was harmful to their health. Eight years later, one group of participants was 43% more likely to have died—the people who had a lot of stress and believed that stress was bad for them. Those who had a lot of stress but did not believe it was harmful actually had the lowest risk of dying!

According to McGonigal, the way we think about stress is important because, "Your body believes you." In fact, our mind and attitude can have beneficial effects on our health and may help prevent some kinds of serious illness. In a study at Harvard, researchers taught participants to believe that signs of stress—a faster heartbeat, for example—were the body's way of preparing them to meet a challenge. Under stress, most people's blood vessels become **narrower**. That makes it harder for blood to flow and may contribute to heart disease. But the blood vessels of the study participants stayed open and relaxed, simply because they thought about stress in a different way.

McGonigal also points to a study of the connection between stress and human contact. Researchers from the University at Buffalo studied people who had experienced very stressful events during the past year. Surprisingly, if they had spent a lot of time helping others, they had no increased risk of dying. Compare that to a 30% increase for those who had not helped others. It seems that enjoyable activities such as giving a friend a ride or babysitting a neighbor's child can help us stay healthy even under stress.

**stress** worry and tension due to difficulties in life
**enemy** the person(s) on the opposite side in a struggle
**participants** people who volunteer for a research study
**narrower** having a smaller distance from one side to the other

**Appreciating the beauty of nature can help foster a positive attitude.**

# GOAL  Explain an Idea Using Details

## Communication

**A** Discuss the questions in pairs.

1. How can a sick person make other people sick? Think of three ways.

2. The last time you got sick, how do you think you caught the illness?

**B** In pairs, discuss how each action can prevent the spread of disease. Add your own idea.

covering your nose and mouth

staying home when you're sick

washing your hands often

exercising and eating healthy foods

using clean dishes for eating and drinking

your idea: _____

Coughing or sneezing sends germs into the air.

Washing your hands removes germs from your skin.

Yes, and other people breathe in the germs.

I always wash my hands before I eat.

## Writing

**WRITING SKILL:** Using Supporting Details

A good topic sentence gives the main idea of a paragraph. In addition, a good paragraph includes details to support, or give more information about, the main idea.

Some types of supporting details:

descriptions        examples        explanations        facts        reasons

**C** Underline the topic sentence in the following paragraph. Then answer the questions below.

Although there are several ways to prevent the spread of disease, staying home when you are sick may be the best way. When you stay home, no one at school or at work has contact with your germs. Going to work or school and covering your mouth when you cough is less effective than staying at home. Some of your germs are still sent into the air when you talk and breathe. And washing your hands after every cough or sneeze may be the least effective way to keep other people healthy. It is not possible to wash your hands that many times in a day.

1. What is the topic of the paragraph? (i.e., What is the paragraph about?)

_____

2. What is the controlling idea? (i.e., What does the paragraph say about the topic?)

_____

Complete the chart with supporting details from the paragraph in **C**.

| Reason to stay at home when sick | Reason why covering one's mouth is less effective | Reason why washing one's hands often may be the least effective |
|---|---|---|
|  |  |  |

E Choose one of the topics and write a paragraph about it. Use your own ideas. Remember to include a good topic sentence and a few details to support it.

exercise                having a positive attitude                healthy foods

✓ **GOAL CHECK** Explain an Idea Using Details

In pairs, follow the steps.

1. Tell your partner about your paragraph. Which topic did you choose, and why?

2. Talk about your main idea and the details you included.

**A sneeze in slow motion**

# TEDTALKS

## LIVING BEYOND LIMITS

**A** Read the quotation. Discuss the question in pairs.

*"If your life were a book, and you were the author, how would you want your story to go? That's the question that changed my life forever."*

—Amy Purdy

How do you think this question might have changed Amy Purdy's life?

**B** Watch the TED Talk. Circle the correct words to complete the sentences.

1. Amy Purdy grew up in *Las Vegas* / *Los Angeles*.

2. Purdy's disease caused her to lose parts of her body and the hearing in her *left* / *right* ear.

3. On her 21st birthday, Purdy received a new *foot* / *kidney* from her father.

4. Purdy won two *gold* / *silver* World Cup medals for snowboarding.

5. Purdy has learned to rely on her *parents* / *imagination*.

**C** Complete each sentence from the video with one word.

1. At the age of 19, a day after I ▮▮▮▮▮▮▮ high school, I moved to a place where it snowed.

2. I went home from work early one day with what I thought was the ▮▮▮▮▮▮▮.

3. When my parents wheeled me out of the ▮▮▮▮▮▮▮, I felt like I had been pieced back together.

4. I was absolutely ▮▮▮▮▮▮ and emotionally broken.

5. And that is when it dawned on me … I could be as ▮▮▮▮▮▮ as I wanted!

6. And that is when a new ▮▮▮▮▮▮ in my life began.

**D** Read the quotation. Then discuss the questions with a partner.

*"And this is when I learned that our borders and our obstacles can only do two things: One, stop us in our tracks; or two, force us to get creative."*

—Amy Purdy

1. What were two or three obstacles Purdy faced after her illness?

2. Before she went snowboarding again, what did Purdy imagine?

3. How did Purdy get the "feet" she needed in order to snowboard again?

**AMY PURDY**
Professional Snowboarder

Amy Purdy's **idea worth spreading** is that you can draw inspiration from life's obstacles. Watch Purdy's TED TALK on TED.com.

National Geographic Explorer
Sarah McNair-Landry
exploring the Northwest
Passage of Canada

**Look at the photo and answer the questions:**

**1** What phrase best describes this photo?

**2** What do you think of when you hear the word *challenge*?

## UNIT 5 GOALS

**A.** Talk about Facing Challenges

**B.** Describe Past Accomplishments

**C.** Use *Too* and *Enough* to Talk about Abilities

**D.** Discuss Steps Toward a Goal

**E.** Describe a Personal Challenge

59

**GOAL** Talk about Facing Challenges

## Vocabulary

A Read about two people's challenges.

| Physical Challenge | Mental Challenge |
|---|---|
| I absolutely love a challenge! Doing something difficult makes me feel alive. Recently I set a goal for myself: To run a marathon and make it to the finish line. I trained almost every day before the marathon, and I felt like I was making progress toward my goal. Last month, I achieved the goal with a competitive time! | Although it might not seem like a significant challenge to some people, reading is quite difficult for me, especially when I need to do a lot of it. Last year, I convinced my parents to hire a reading tutor to help me. I learned ways to deal with large amounts of reading homework, and I hope the result will be better grades this year. |

B Write each word in blue next to the correct meaning.

1. _____ a target you hope to reach

2. _____ something new or different that requires effort

3. _____ introduces a statement with a contrast

4. _____ to succeed in making something happen

5. _____ large enough to be important

6. _____ improvement over time

7. _____ something that happens because of something else

8. _____ to give an impression or appear a certain way

9. _____ to manage or handle a situation well

10. _____ to persuade someone to do something

**Marathon runners in Montreal, Canada**

## Grammar

| The Past Continuous and Simple Past | |
| --- | --- |
| Use the past continuous to talk about something that was in progress at a specific time in the past.<br><br>Form the past continuous with *was / were* + the *-ing* form of a verb. | I saw Sasha at the library yesterday. He **was working** on his assignment.<br>We **weren't watching** a movie at 8:00 last night. We **were studying** for a test. |
| Use the simple past to talk about completed actions or situations. | Edmund Hillary and Tenzing Norgay **climbed** Mount Everest. |
| Use *when* for an action in the simple past and *while* with the past continuous to say that something happened when another event was in progress. | It **was raining** very hard **when Rita crossed** the finish line.<br>Sara **got** a text message **while she was talking** with her professor. |
| Use a comma after a time clause when it begins a sentence. | **While Ben was writing** his paper, the computer stopped working. |

**C** Complete each sentence with *when* or *while*.

1. Martina was looking for a job _____ I met her for the first time.

2. The mountain climbers were resting _____ the storm began.

3. My phone rang six times _____ I was working on my project.

4. _____ he was visiting Quito, Justin practiced his Spanish.

**D** Complete the sentences. Use the simple past or past continuous form of the verbs.

1. Yesterday, I _____ (convince) my best friend to compete in a 5k race.

2. Maria _____ (deal with) health problems when she quit her job last October.

3. My parents _____ (look) for new jobs when they met.

4. The professor _____ (seem) tired in class last week.

5. We _____ (make) progress with the project when the class ended.

6. At the gymnastics competition, Leo _____ (achieve) the highest score.

 **GOAL CHECK** Talk about Facing Challenges

Tell a partner about a challenge you have faced in your life.

1. What was happening in your life at that time?

2. What did you do? Do you think you dealt with the challenge well?

> My father lost his job last year while studying for exams.

> That's awful! What did you and your family do?

**B** | **GOAL** Describe Past Accomplishments

## Listening

**A** Read the information in the box. Discuss the questions in pairs.

> **Dr. Jenny Daltry: Wildlife Conservationist and Ecologist**
>
> Cambodian Crocodile Conservation Programme
> Antiguan Racer Conservation Project
> Sustainable Lansan Project

1. What do you think it means to *conserve* wildlife?
2. What kinds of wildlife do you think Jenny Daltry is interested in?
3. What kinds of challenges do you think Jenny Daltry might face in her work?

**WORD FOCUS**

If an animal is **endangered**, its population is so small that it might die out. An animal is **extinct** when none of its kind is alive.

**B** 🎧 21 Listen to the conversation. Circle the correct letter.

1. What is the man working on?

   **a.** a conservation project
   **b.** a presentation assignment

2. What did Daltry convince people in Cambodia to do?

   **a.** to care about the crocodiles
   **b.** to kill fewer crocodiles

3. What causes problems for the Antiguan Racer snakes?

   **a.** progress on the island
   **b.** people, rats, and bad weather

4. Where does the *lansan* tree grow?

   **a.** in the Caribbean
   **b.** in Cambodia

The Siamese crocodile is one of the species Dr. Jenny Daltry is working to protect.

**C** 🎧 21 Listen again. Complete the statements with two or three words you hear.

1. The assignment is to learn about someone who _____ .

2. As a result of Daltry's work, the Cambodian government decided to protect _____ acres of forest.

3. She saved an animal species, and it's _____ that people don't even like.

4. They found _____, and it doesn't hurt the trees.

**WORD FOCUS**

To **achieve a goal** means to succeed in doing something you hoped to do.

An **accomplishment** is something special that you achieve.

**D** 🎧 22 Listen to these words that end in -ed.

> **PRONUNCIATION:** Words that end in -ed
>
> | /t/ | /d/ | /ɪd/ |
> |---|---|---|
> | help   helped | listen   listened | start   started |

**E** 🎧 23 Listen, repeat, and check (✓) the column of the sound made by the -ed ending.

| Present | Simple Past | /t/ | /d/ | /ɪd/ |
|---|---|---|---|---|
| convince | convinced | ____ | ____ | ____ |
| protect | protected | ____ | ____ | ____ |
| discover | discovered | ____ | ____ | ____ |
| need | needed | ____ | ____ | ____ |
| close | closed | ____ | ____ | ____ |
| walk | walked | ____ | ____ | ____ |

**F** Write down ten regular present verbs that end in /t/ or /d/. Say a verb. Ask your partner to say it in the past.

## Communication

**G** Use the ideas in the box to talk about Jenny Daltry and her accomplishments. Remember to pronounce verbs that end in -ed correctly.

> | | |
> |---|---|
> | convince people to care for crocodiles | discover a group of crocodiles |
> | save a kind of snake in the Caribbean | try different ways to get *lansan* tree sap |
> | walk into areas of Cambodia | work on three conservation projects |

 **GOAL CHECK** Describe Past Accomplishments

> I practiced a lot, and now I play the violin pretty well.

1. In your notebook, write notes about something you achieved and how you achieved it.

2. Tell a partner about your accomplishment. Give details about how you did it and how you felt.

## C GOAL Use *Too* and *Enough* to Talk about Abilities

### Language Expansion: Phrasal Verbs

**A** Read the article.

Subaru Takahashi was only 14 years old when he set out on an amazing adventure. His goal was to sail from Tokyo to San Francisco—alone. Subaru grew up near the sea and loved sailing. His parents thought he was old enough to sail alone, and they helped him buy a boat. He left on July 22. At first, the trip was easy. Then, after three weeks, his batteries broke down, so he didn't have any lights. He had to watch out for big ships at night, because it was too dark to see his boat. Five days later, his radio stopped working. Subaru was really alone then, but he didn't give up. His progress was very slow, but he kept on sailing. He almost ran out of food, and he was not fast enough to catch fish. He put up with hot sun and strong wind. On September 13, Subaru sailed into San Francisco. He was the youngest person ever to sail alone across the Pacific Ocean.

**Subaru Takahashi, the youngest person to sail alone across the Pacific Ocean**

**B** Match each phrasal verb in blue with its meaning.

1. set out _____
2. give up _____
3. watch out _____
4. grow up _____
5. keep on _____
6. run out of _____
7. put up with _____
8. break down _____

a. accept something bad without being upset
b. change from a child to an adult
c. finish the amount of something that you have
d. leave on a trip
e. be very careful
f. stop trying
g. continue trying
h. stop working

**C** MY WORLD Would you have been brave enough to sail across the ocean alone at the age of 14? What brave things have you done in your life? Discuss in pairs.

### Grammar

**D** Read these sentences and the questions that follow. Circle **Y** for *yes* or **N** for *no*.

1. "He was <u>old enough</u> to sail alone."
   Could he sail alone?      **Y**    **N**

2. "He was <u>not fast enough</u> to catch fish."
   Could he catch fish?      **Y**    **N**

3. "It was <u>too dark</u> to see his boat."
   Could people see his boat?      **Y**    **N**

## Enough, Not Enough, Too + Adjective

| adjective + *enough* = the amount that you want | He was **old enough** to sail alone. |
| --- | --- |
| *not* + adjective + *enough* = less than the amount that you want | He was **not fast enough** to catch fish. |
| *too* + adjective = more than the amount you want | His boat was **too dark** to see. |

 Complete the sentences. Use *enough*, *not enough*, or *too*, and the adjective.

1. Subaru's boat was _____ (big) for two people.

2. A boat is _____ (expensive) for me to buy because I don't have much money.

3. Crossing the ocean alone is _____ (difficult) for most people to do.

4. My parents say I'm _____ (old) to travel alone. I have to wait until I'm 18.

5. I think Subaru's trip was _____ (dangerous) for a young person. His parents should not have let him go alone.

6. A trip to San Francisco by plane is a fun adventure, and it's _____ (safe) for my family and me. Maybe we'll go there for our next vacation.

## Conversation

**F** 🎧 24 Close your book and listen to the conversation. What does Lisa need to do before she can climb the mountain?

**Lisa:** Do you know what I want to do next summer? My goal is to climb Black Mountain.

**Mari:** Are you serious? Black Mountain is too hard to climb. Don't you need special equipment?

**Lisa:** I already asked about it. I just need good boots.

**Mari:** And you're not strong enough to climb a mountain!

**Lisa:** You're right, I can't do it now. But I'll go hiking every weekend. Next summer, I'll be fit enough to climb the mountain.

**Mari:** Well, I like hiking. I'll go with you sometimes!

**SPEAKING STRATEGY**

You can show surprise in an informal conversation by saying:

*Are you serious?*

*Are you kidding me?*

 **GOAL CHECK**
### Use *Too* and *Enough* to talk about abilities

Write down six things you want to do. In pairs, discuss whether you can do these things now. Are you old enough to do them? Are they affordable or too expensive?

## D GOAL Discuss Steps Toward a Goal

### Reading

**A** **MY WORLD** Are young people in middle school or high school old enough to do good things for the environment? Discuss your ideas in pairs.

**B** Read the article. Answer the questions.

1. What first inspired the sisters?
_____

2. What challenge or problem are they facing?
_____

3. What lesson does Green School Bali teach its students?
_____

**C** Match the details with the ideas they support.

1. _____ Gandhi, Princess Diana, and Mandela
2. _____ empty plastic bottles and cups
3. _____ a ban on plastic bags
4. _____ bringing reusable bags to shops
5. _____ people in Bali and global teams

a. kinds of plastic garbage
b. not working by yourself
c. things the organization is doing
d. significant people
e. something other countries have done

**D** Work with a small group. Discuss the questions.

1. What big problem do the sisters want to deal with?

2. According to the third paragraph, what is their goal for now?

3. What steps have the sisters taken toward their goal? Make a list.

### ✓ GOAL CHECK

Follow the steps with your group.

1. What problem is everyone in your group concerned about? It might be a global problem or a local problem in your country or city.

2. What is a realistic goal you might set to try to deal with the problem?

3. What are 3–4 small steps you could take toward achieving your goal? Make a list.

# Making a Difference: Bali

It started with a lesson at their school about significant people. Two sisters, Melati and Isabel Wijsen, were only 10 and 12 years old at the time. They were **inspired** after learning about people such as Mahatma Gandhi, Princess Diana, and Nelson Mandela. So they asked themselves: What can two girls in Bali, Indonesia do to make a difference in the world?

The answer was all around them on the island. When they walked

to school or swam in the ocean, they saw **plastic** garbage. Empty water bottles, plastic cups and **straws** seemed to be everywhere. In fact, like many places, Bali produces an enormous amount of plastic garbage every day. That includes the thin plastic bags that many shops give to their customers. When the girls learned that those bags had already been **banned** in several countries, they decided it was a good place for them to start. "If they can do it, we can do it," says Melati.

The result is a youth organization called Bye-Bye Plastic Bags. Their goal, for now, is to make one village completely plastic-free. In order to achieve that goal, they bring reusable shopping bags to local shops every Saturday. They have also taken several other steps; for example, creating booklets to educate children about the garbage problem, making **devices** to collect plastic from streams and rivers, and convincing many hotels and restaurants to reduce waste. Isabel points out that, "You can't do it by yourself." Now, the team of young people in Bali have been joined by several global teams working to reduce plastic garbage in countries around the world.

Melati and Isabel attend Green School Bali, where students are taught to become the leaders of today. The sisters decided they did not want to wait until they were adults to become significant people. Although the challenge of dealing with plastic garbage is huge, these young people in Indonesia are making progress and making a difference.

**inspire** give new ideas or strong feelings, enthusiasm
**plastic** a light but strong material made from oil
**straw** a long, narrow tube for drinking
**banned** not allowed, illegal
**device** an object used to do a certain job

Beaches like Atuh Beach at Nusa Penida Island are affected by plastic garbage in Bali.

# E GOAL Describe a Personal Challenge

## Communication

**A** People face challenges for different reasons, but there is usually some reward when they accomplish their goal. What are three or four challenges in life that cannot be avoided? (For example, it can be a challenge to get along well with all of our family members or neighbors.) What are the rewards if we face those challenges? Discuss these questions in pairs.

**B** Tell your partner about two or three challenges in your life that you chose for yourself. Why did you choose to do those things?

## Writing

**WRITING SKILL:** Using Specific Information

When you describe something in writing, specific information helps your reader imagine and understand your ideas. The more interesting your details are, the more your writing will engage your reader. Specific information might include:

- dates or times  • descriptions  • locations  • people's reactions
- step-by-step actions

> Babysitting seemed like an easy job, but on that **Saturday afternoon**, Adam got bored quickly. First, he **complained**. Then, he **cried loudly for several minutes**. At first, I didn't know how to deal with **a bored two-year-old boy**, but then I had an idea. I **went into the kitchen** and came back with **a big bowl of apples, pears, and limes**. Adam looked **surprised**...

**C** In pairs, rank the information from 1 (most specific) to 3 (least specific). Discuss your reasons.

1. _____ children    _____ two-year-old boys    _____ two-year-olds

2. _____ vehicles    _____ airplanes    _____ transportation

**D** Choose one of the challenges you told your partner about in **A**. Follow the steps.

1. Write the challenge as one sentence in your notebook.

2. Under the sentence, list key words about what happened. How did you face the challenge? What happened after that?

**E** Use your sentence and notes from **D** to write a complete paragraph about a challenging experience from your own life. Finish the topic sentence below or write your own. Then, add details with interesting specific information.

**Topic sentence:** When I was _____ years old, I decided to _____

_____ .

**Details:** It was a challenge because _____

_____ .

**F** Exchange paragraphs with a partner.

1. Read your partner's paragraph and underline the parts that were most interesting to you.

2. Tell your partner which parts you underlined and why.

3. Ask your partner one or two questions about the paragraph.

**G** Rewrite your paragraph. You might want to add a few more details to make the paragraph more interesting or to answer the questions from your partner.

✓ **GOAL CHECK** Describe a Personal Challenge

Read your paragraph aloud to a small group. After each person reads, tell him or her which information was interesting to you. Ask questions.

**British artist Stephen Wiltshire draws, from memory, a panoramic view of Mexico City, Mexico.**

# VIDEO JOURNAL

## SUCCESS STORY: RECYCLING IN THE PHILIPPINES

**A** Discuss the questions in pairs.

1. At home or at school, do you separate garbage from things to be recycled?

2. What kinds of things are usually recycled?

**B** Read the information.

Heather Koldewey could easily see the challenge. As a marine biologist, she knew there were fewer fish living in the reefs near the Philippines. One problem was too much fishing. Another problem was harmful plastic garbage in the ocean, including plastic fishing nets. Koldewey wanted to get the local people involved in marine conservation, but in poor communities, people have real and immediate needs that take priority. How could she convince them to care for the environment more?

Koldewey and her team members like Amado "Madz" Blanco have come up with one solution to these problems. Net-Works collects plastic fishing nets and exports them from the Philippines to Europe. There, they are made into nylon yarn for carpet. This process has removed 18 tonnes (19.84 US tons) of nets from just one island and provided much-needed money for islanders.

Fishing nets in the ocean affect marine habitats. Here some marine plants are growing on their strings.

**C** Write each word in blue next to its meaning.

1. _____ brings things together in one place

2. _____ natural structures in the ocean where many fish live

3. _____ related to the present

4. _____ long thread usually used for weaving

5. _____ sells products or materials to another country

6. _____ groups of people living in a certain area

7. _____ a covering of soft material laid over a floor

**D** Watch the video and check (✓) the things you see.

☐ a reef with few fish     ☐ small fishing boats

☐ plastic in the ocean     ☐ a large truck

☐ tourists at a beach hotel     ☐ colorful t-shirts

**E** Watch again. Complete each statement with one or two words that you hear.

1. "As a marine biologist, I quickly realized I really wanted to do something that was going to make _____."

2. "It's globally _____, this place— from a marine biodiversity point of view."

3. "Many of our team are also _____ organizers—people who can talk to people."

4. "What is so inspiring for me is actually seeing what communities who have so very little can actually do and _____ change they can make."

5. "People can easily buy into something that is supported with _____ science."

**F** In pairs, list all of the steps you saw or heard about in the video for recycling fishing nets.

**G** In pairs, take turns describing the steps in the net recycling process.

REAL LANGUAGE

If you **buy into** an idea, you believe in it.

# Transitions

**Kosavar Bosnian bride preparing for traditional wedding in Donje Ljubinje located in the Shar Mountains beween Kosovo and Macedonia**

## UNIT 6 GOALS

**A.** Talk about Different Stages in Your Life

**B.** Talk about the Best Age to do Something

**C.** Ask Questions to Get More Information

**D.** Discuss Changes Caused by Technology

**E.** Describe an Important Transition in Your Life

# A   GOAL  Talk about Different Stages in Your Life

## Vocabulary

**A** Read the information.

**Night sky observed through a telescope**

Nadia Drake is a writer for National Geographic and the daughter of a famous astronomer. As a child, she attended lectures and other events with her dad. It may have been her relationship with him that eventually led her to develop her own love of astronomy. Astronomy isn't Drake's only interest, though. She also has a PhD in genetics, and before she earned that degree, she had worked as a professional ballet dancer. Then, she realized that writing about science was the career she wanted. Once she had chosen this direction for her career, many interesting opportunities opened up for her. For example, Drake recently wrote an article about a photographer who used cameras to learn about wild rainforest animals in Peru. "This is basically my dream job," she says. The negative part of the job might be that her schedule is not very regular. The positive part is the writing, so she is happy with the choice she made.

**B** Write each word in blue next to the correct definition.

1. _____ something that happens

2. _____ good

3. _____ became aware

4. _____ way something is going

5. _____ job or occupation

6. _____ bad

7. _____ grow over time

8. _____ chances to do something

9. _____ connection, friendship

10. _____ finally, after some time

## Grammar

| **The Past Perfect** | |
|---|---|
| The past perfect describes a past event that happened before another point in the past. Form the past perfect with *had* + the past participle of a verb. | When I met Franz, he **had** already **changed** jobs several times. Before she started primary school, Luisa **had learned** both Italian and French. |
| The past perfect is often used to explain why a past event or situation happened. | I wasn't worried about meeting the graduation requirements because I **had gotten** several extra credits. |
| With *before* or *after*, we often use the simple past instead of the past perfect, since the time relationship is clear. | Luckily, my brother **realized** he hated math **before** he declared his major. |

**C** Complete each sentence using the past perfect form of the verb in parentheses.

1. Before Nadia Drake earned her degree, she _____ (be) a ballet dancer.

2. Her father _____ (love) astronomy and Nadia also developed a love for it.

3. The teacher _____ (realize) the topic was difficult, so she explained it carefully.

4. She _____ (plan) to have a different career, but she eventually became a software writer.

5. We weren't surprised when the road changed direction because we _____ (study) the map.

**D** Discuss the sentences in **C** with a partner. In each sentence, which past event happened first? Which event happened second?

**E** Interview a partner using these questions and any others you may have.

1. Tell me about a positive experience or event in your life. When did it happen? What had happened before this experience?

2. How did the positive experience change the direction of your life?

3. Tell me about a negative experience or event in your life. When did it happen? What had happened before this experience?

4. What did you realize about yourself after this negative experience or event?

> I was in a school play last year. I had been pretty lonely, and it was an opportunity to make friends.

> I had always wanted to do the same things as my older sister did, but when I was 6, I learned a hard lesson.

   Other questions: _____
   _____
   _____

**F** Follow the steps to prepare for an informal presentation.

1. Think about your answers in **E** and prepare to speak about your life for 1–2 minutes.

2. Write key words, dates, and a few other details. Try to use the past perfect and some of the vocabulary words.

| Key Words | Dates | Details |
|---|---|---|
| _____ | _____ | _____ |
| _____ | _____ | _____ |
| _____ | _____ | _____ |

# ✓ GOAL CHECK
## Talk about Different Stages in Your Life

Get together with 2–3 other students. Give your presentation and answer any questions your classmates may have. Speak naturally and use your notes only when necessary.

# B GOAL Talk about the Best Age to Do Something

## Listening

**A** Discuss the question in pairs. Add your own idea.

In your opinion, when does someone become an adult?

- when they graduate
- when they have their own home
- when they have a child
- when they start their career

**B** 🎧 26 Listen to a conversation between two friends. Circle **T** for *true* or **F** for *false*.

| | | | |
|---|---|---|---|
| 1. The man is helping the woman with her savings plan and her taxes. | | T | F |
| 2. The woman hopes to help her parents financially. | | T | F |
| 3. The man will help the woman with her finances again next year. | | T | F |

**C** 🎧 26 Listen again. How would the two speakers complete the statements?

1. The woman thinks she is an adult because

_____.

2. The man has a different idea of adulthood because _____.

3. The woman thinks her parents don't need her help with _____.

4. The man has a positive idea about _____.

**D** In pairs, talk about how people from your culture usually help their parents.

WORD FOCUS

Your **finances** (n) have to do with your money.

Other forms are **financial** (adj) and **financially** (adv).

## Pronunciation: The Schwa Sound /ə/ in Unstressed Syllables

**E** 🎧 27 Listen to the words. Notice the vowel sound of the unstressed syllables in blue. This is the schwa sound /ə/, and it's the most common vowel sound in English.

infant     lettuce     children     population     adult

**F** 🎧 28 Listen and repeat. Circle the unstressed syllables with the /ə/ sound.

| | | | | |
|---|---|---|---|---|
| alone | lesson | person | banana | parents |
| paper | challenge | language | national | chicken |

Graduation day at the University of Texas in San Antonio, Texas

## Conversation

**G** 🎧 29 Close your book and listen to the conversation. How old is Jamal?

**Andrea:** Did you hear the big news? Jamal is getting his own apartment!

**Kim:** Seriously? But he's 19! That's too young to get your own place.

**Andrea:** Oh, I don't know about that.

**Kim:** Do you think he's old enough?

**Andrea:** Well, he's mature, and he's had a part-time job since he was 17.

**Kim:** That's true... but I think he should wait a few years.

**Andrea:** Really? What do you think is the best age to live on your own?

**Kim:** I think people should get their own place after they've finished college.

**Andrea:** That's a good point. I plan to live with my parents while I'm in college.

> **REAL LANGUAGE**
>
> You can say **Oh, I don't know about that** to disagree politely with someone.

**H** Practice the conversation in pairs. Switch roles and repeat.

**I** In pairs, use your own ideas to complete the table below in your notebook. Then, write two conversations about Jorge and Melissa using the conversation in **G** as an example.

| **"Jorge is too old to change jobs."** | **"Melissa is too young to start her own business."** |
|---|---|
| Age: _____<br><br>Reasons why it is or isn't OK<br><br>_____<br>_____ | Age: _____<br><br>Reasons why it is or isn't OK<br><br>_____<br>_____ |
| The best age for this is _____ | The best age for this is _____ |

**J** Read the opinions. How old do you think each person is?

1. "He's too old to play soccer."
2. "He's too young to travel alone."
3. "She's too old to dance."
4. "She's too young to drive a car."
5. "She's too old to learn a new language."
6. "He's too old to get married."

**K** **MY WORLD** Tell a partner two things you think you are too old to do. What are two things you think you are too young to do?

 **GOAL CHECK**
## Talk about the Best Age to do Something

Look at your answers in **J**. Compare answers in pairs and explain your opinions. What is the best age for each of these things? Do you know someone who does these things at an unusual age?

> The best age to play any sport is in your teens or twenties.

> I don't know—some professional athletes are in their forties!

# GOAL Ask Questions to Get More Information

## Language Expansion: Adjectives for Age

**A** Do you know someone who fits any of these descriptions? Who? Share your answers in pairs. Use the adjectives in the box to help you.

| | |
|---|---|
| youthful | older, but with the energy of a young person (positive) |
| childish | older, but acting like a child (negative) |
| mature | old enough to be responsible and make good decisions |
| in his / her twenties | between 20 and 29 (also *in his teens, thirties, forties,* etc.) |
| middle-aged | not young or old (about 40–60) |
| retired | stopped working full time (often after 65) |
| elderly | looking and acting old |

**B** Talk with a partner about people you know. How old are they? Describe them with adjectives from **A**.

family members
friends
neighbors
other people in your community

## Grammar

| *How* + Adjective or Adverb | |
|---|---|
| Adjectives give information about nouns. Use *How* + adjective to ask a question about a descriptive adjective. | **A:** Lenora is **mature** for her age. <br> **B: How mature** is she? <br> **A:** She's mature enough to babysit my son. |
| Adverbs give information about verbs. Use *How* + adverb to ask a question about an adverb. | **A:** I learn **quickly**. <br> **B: How quickly** do you learn? <br> **A:** I learned to ride a bicycle in one day! |
| Common adjectives: *young, old, early, clean, happy, difficult, polite, serious* <br> Common adverbs: *well, badly, often, rarely, quickly, slowly, easily, carefully* | |

Women at different stages of life wait for the event to start.

**C** Unscramble the questions. In pairs, take turns asking the questions.

1. English / how / do / speak / well / you _____?

2. you / how / are / old _____?

3. can / fast / you / how / type _____?

4. you / how / tall / are _____?

5. your / family / how / often / move / does _____?

**D** Complete the conversations. Write questions using *how*.

1. **A:** I think Mr. Chen is too elderly to live alone.

   **B:** He doesn't look old to me. _____?

2. **A:** My brother failed his driver's license test six times because he drives so badly.

   **B:** Wow! _____?

3. **A:** I can't go to the movie tonight. My first class is very early tomorrow.

   **B:** That's too bad. _____?

4. **A:** I don't want to get my own apartment. It's much too expensive.

   **B:** Really _____?

5. **A:** I haven't finished reading the assignment for tomorrow. I guess I read too slowly.

   **B:** That's a problem. _____?

## Conversation

**E** 🎧 30 Close your book and listen to the conversation. What did Erik get?

**Mrs. Ryan:** My son Erik just got his first credit card.

**Mrs. Chen:** Is that a good idea? He's still a college student.

**Mrs. Ryan:** That's true, but he has always been careful with money.

**Mrs. Chen:** Really? How careful is he?

**Mrs. Ryan:** He's very careful. In high school, he saved enough money to buy a computer.

**Mrs. Chen:** Then maybe he is ready to get a credit card.

**F** In your notebook, write 3–4 adjectives to describe a person you know. Then, write 3–4 things the person does and describe how the person does them.

**SPEAKING STRATEGY**

**Disagreeing Politely**
*That's true, but…*

*You're right, but…*

*I see what you mean, but…*

## GOAL CHECK
### Ask Questions to Get More Information

In pairs, take turns describing the person you chose in **F** and how he or she does things. Use questions with *How* to get as much information as possible.

> My grandmother is quite lovable. She makes new friends easily.

> How easily does she make new friends?

## D

**GOAL** Discuss Changes Caused by Technology

### Reading

**A** In pairs, discuss how you use these technologies.

> apps for your phone   online shopping
> smartphone

**B** Read the article and answer the questions.

1. What kind of technology is mentioned in the first paragraph?
   _____

2. What two technologies are mentioned in the second and third paragraphs?
   _____

3. What does Bright Simons's invention do?
   _____

4. Why does Shapshak think innovation is not happening in the developed world?
   _____

**C** Read the article again. Circle **T** for *true* or **F** for *false*. Make the false statements true.

1. Toby Shapshak is an engineer from South Africa.          T   F

2. M-Pesa helps people pay bills and buy groceries.          T   F

3. Bright Simons's invention is a smartphone app.          T   F

4. African inventions can help people worldwide.          T   F

 **GOAL CHECK**

Join another pair and discuss the questions.

1. What do you think life was like for many African people before they had the innovations from the article?

2. How is life better for many African people now?

3. How has your life changed because of new technology?

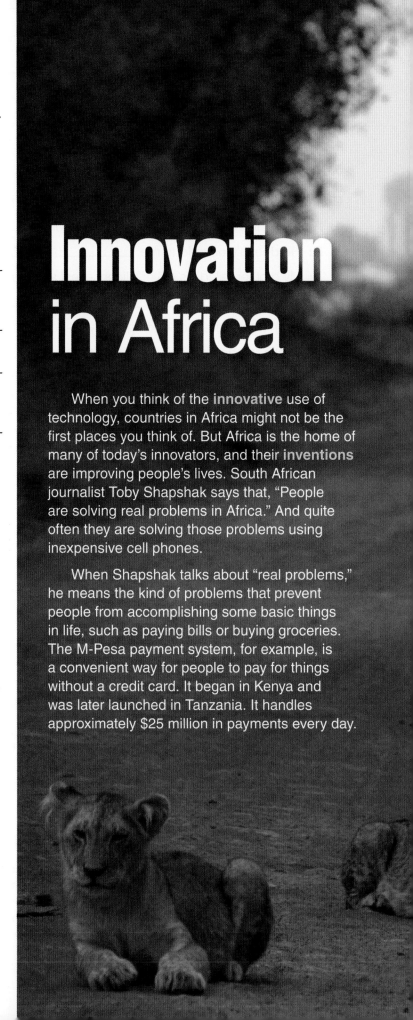

# Innovation in Africa

When you think of the **innovative** use of technology, countries in Africa might not be the first places you think of. But Africa is the home of many of today's innovators, and their **inventions** are improving people's lives. South African journalist Toby Shapshak says that, "People are solving real problems in Africa." And quite often they are solving those problems using inexpensive cell phones.

When Shapshak talks about "real problems," he means the kind of problems that prevent people from accomplishing some basic things in life, such as paying bills or buying groceries. The M-Pesa payment system, for example, is a convenient way for people to pay for things without a credit card. It began in Kenya and was later launched in Tanzania. It handles approximately $25 million in payments every day.

Another cellphone-based service called iCow sends its users daily information about how to care for **dairy** animals. This creative use of technology is very helpful in Kenya, where dairy farming is an important industry.

In the Republic of Ghana, an African inventor named Bright Simons developed a way for **consumers** to check the freshness of prescription medicines. People buying a medicine simply send a set of numbers from the package to an SMS number. They then receive a message with information. This lets them know if the medicine will be **effective**. The technology works, and it can save lives.

Perhaps the best part about all three of these services is that they use SMS technology. This means that they work with any cell phone and that having an expensive smartphone is not necessary for using them.

Shapshak **asserts** that true innovation isn't happening much in other parts of the world since people are too busy playing video games or using social media. Inventions that are improving and even saving lives in Africa are ideas that can benefit people everywhere. Says Shapshak about the people there, "I don't believe that the gold is under the ground. I believe we are the gold."

**innovative**  new and original
**inventions**  new things that people create
**dairy**  related to milk
**consumers**  people who buy and use products
**effective**  something is *effective* if it works well
**asserts**  states an opinion or belief

**Lion cubs rest in the Nairobi national park in Kenya with the Nairobi skyline visible behind them.**

# GOAL  Describe an Important Transition in Your Life

## Communication

| from child to teenager |
| --- |
| from teenager to adult |
| from single to married |
| from studying to working |
| from non-parent to parent |
| from middle age to old age |

**A** What do you know about each life transition in the box? Tell a partner what you think happens or what you have experienced.

> As a teenager, I had different friends.

> Me, too. I spent more time with the friends I had made in high school.

**B** Discuss the questions in pairs.

1. Who does the cleaning and other chores at your house?
2. How often do you do your own laundry?
3. When was the last time you bought groceries?
4. Are you old enough to vote?

## Writing

> **WRITING SKILL:** Using Time Expressions
>
> Time expressions help your reader understand when different events happened.
> **As soon as** *he realized his mistake, he apologized for it.*
> This means there was no delay. He didn't wait until later to apologize.
>
> *We had* **already** *read about Einstein's early life, so we didn't need to hear a lecture about it.*
> The word *already* emphasizes that the reading happened before the lecture.
>
> **Example time expressions:** *until   by +* date or time   *never   last week / month / year*
> *after that   eventually   a week / month / year ago*

**C** Read the sample paragraph and discuss the questions below with a partner.

1. What is the topic sentence in this paragraph?
2. What two examples support the topic sentence?
3. How did the writer feel about this transition in his or her life?
4. How do the bolded expressions help you understand the writer's meaning?

When I finished middle school and started high school, my parents began to give me more responsibilities. I had **already** started to wash some of my own clothes, but **that summer** it became my responsibility to do laundry for the whole family. My other chore was buying groceries for my elderly grandmother. I went to visit her **twice a week**, and I asked her what she needed from the grocery store. She gave me the money, and I returned with her food, soap, and other necessities. It wasn't hard to do and I enjoyed spending time with her. I also began to feel good about doing my family's laundry each week. It felt like I was moving from childhood toward adulthood.

 Complete the questionnaire. Write answers in your notebook.

### QUESTIONNAIRE

1. Where do you live now?
2. How many times have you moved in your life?
3. As a child, what did you dream of being or doing when you got older?
4. What do you dream of being or doing now?
5. When did you meet your best friend or friends?
6. What are some of the most important personal relationships in your life?
7. What event in your life do you think changed you the most?

**E** Read your answers to the questionnaire—especially to question 7. Write a well-organized paragraph about a life transition and make sure it includes the following:

- a good topic sentence
- plenty of interesting details
- time expressions to show when things happened

## ✓ GOAL CHECK
### Describe an Important Transition in your Life

Follow the steps in pairs.

1. Take turns. Tell your partner about the life transition you described in your paragraph in **E**. Was it easy or difficult for you to write about?
2. Listen carefully while your partner speaks. Ask questions to get more information.

> It was difficult to describe my feelings. It was a long time ago.

> How much do you remember about that time?

**HANS ROSLING**

Professor of Global Health,
Co-founder of Gapminder.org

Hans Rosling's **idea worth spreading** is that
machines have had an incredible effect on the
lives of many—and rich westerners can't just tell
those in the developing world that they can't have
them. Watch Rosling's full TED Talk on TED.com.

# THE MAGIC WASHING MACHINE

**A** In pairs, look at the photo and answer the questions.

   **1.** What is this device? Do you have one in your house?

   **2.** What percent of the world's population do you think has a modern washing machine?

   **3.** How do you think it has changed people's lives?

**B** You will hear these words in the video. Complete the paragraph with the correct words. Not all words will be used.

> **electricity**  flow of energy used as power
> **heat**  cause to become warm or hot
> **load**  put (an amount of something) into or onto something
> **mesmerize**  hold the full attention of
> **time-consuming**  using or needing a large amount of time
> **tough**  very difficult to do or deal with

It's amazing how machines can change the world. Not so many years ago, doing laundry was a (1) ▢▢▢▢▢ job. You needed to (2) ▢▢▢▢▢ the water, add the soap and the clothes, and rub them with your hands for a long, long time. Now, we (3) ▢▢▢▢▢ the washing machine, push the button, and the machine does the rest. It's not (4) ▢▢▢▢▢ at all to get your clothes clean. Of course, a washing machine uses (5) ▢▢▢▢▢ to run.

**C** Watch the TED Talk. Circle the main idea.

   **1.** Washing machines are very popular around the world.

   **2.** Women like to read more than they like to do laundry.

   **3.** When people don't have to do so much hard work, they have time to do things they enjoy and their lives change in positive ways.

**D** Look at the list of devices. Circle the two you think have made the biggest difference in people's lives in the last century.

> air conditioner     cell phone     computer
> dishwasher     microwave oven     vacuum cleaner

**E** In pairs, compare your choices in **D** with a partner. Are there any devices you'd like to add to the list? Think about devices that save on work and give people more time to read and get an education.

A keeper at the International Animal Rescue center takes a group of young orangutans to the forest to learn skills to live in the wild in West Kalimantan Province, Borneo, Indonesia.

## UNIT 7 GOALS

**A.** Discuss Spending Habits

**B.** Talk about Needs and Wants

**C.** Discuss What Makes People's Lives Better

**D.** Talk about Different Lifestyles

**E.** Set Priorities

**GOAL** Discuss Spending Habits

## Vocabulary

**A** Read the article.

**Murano contemporary art, made from glass, is considered a luxury.**

Life is full of choices. Should you buy the latest smartphone, or put your money in a savings account instead? Do you really need that phone, or is it a luxury you can live without? These are questions that are asked every day, and for many people, the answer is to reduce the amount of money they spend in order to increase their happiness.

If you believe the TV commercials, the road to a satisfying life is driven in a beautiful new car. Owning nice things is supposed to produce good feelings in people. Now, though, more people are deciding not to waste their money on a new car when they can easily take the bus or drive an older car. Instead of doing things the usual way—working too much and enjoying life too little—they are choosing to focus on the quality of their lives. They're spending more time doing the things they love and less money buying things they don't need.

**B** Complete each sentence with the correct word in blue.

**1.** If you _____ something, you make it smaller.

**2.** The _____ way is the thing done most often in a certain situation.

**3.** The _____ of something is how good or bad it is.

**4.** If something is a _____, it's very nice, but not necessary.

**5.** When you make a _____, you decide what you want.

**6.** If something is _____, it makes people feel full or happy.

**7.** If you _____ something, you use too much of it for something unimportant.

**8.** The _____ of something is how much of it there is.

**9.** When you _____ something, you make it or cause it to happen.

**10.** If you do one thing _____ of another thing, you do the first thing and not the second.

## Grammar

| Passive Voice (Present Tense) | |
|---|---|
| The passive voice emphasizes the object or receiver of an action. | **Four million cars** are produced every year (by the company). |
| We form the passive with *be* + the past participle of a verb. | A lot of money **is wasted** on things people don't really need. |
| The active voice emphasizes the subject (the agent)—who or what performs an action. | **The company** produces four million cars every year. |
| **Regular Past Participles**<br>created    reduced    achieved | **Irregular Past Participles**<br>made    given    taught |

**C** Complete each sentence with the passive form of the verb in parentheses.

Some things cost a lot because they (1) _____ (produce) by hand.

Murano glass, for example, (2) _____ (make) by hand in Italy.

Many colors (3) _____ (combine) to produce high-quality glass art.

Younger glass artists (4) _____ (teach) by master artists with

years of experience. Tourists like to buy the glass, and some of the best shops

(5) _____ (locate) in Murano, Italy.

**D** Match the beginning of each passive sentence to its ending.

**1.** _____ Food is often wasted

**2.** _____ Energy use is reduced

**3.** _____ Clothing lasts longer

**4.** _____ Towels can be used

**5.** _____ Meals are less expensive

a. when you don't use air conditioning.

b. if it is well taken care of.

c. when people don't eat everything they buy.

d. when they are cooked and eaten at home.

e. for cleaning instead of paper products.

**E** When are you willing to spend or save money? Write the items in the chart.

- the phone I like is made in a new color.
- a new restaurant is opened in my neighborhood.
- a food I like is on sale at the grocery store.
- sneakers are worn by a famous athlete in an ad.
- your idea _____

| I will spend my money when… | I will save my money when… |
| --- | --- |
| | |

✓ **GOAL CHECK** Discuss Spending Habits

Discuss the questions in pairs.

**1.** When are you willing to spend money on something you want?

**2.** When do you decide to save your money instead?

**3.** What do you think many people waste money on?

I want to buy a new phone every time a new feature is added to it!

Sure, but I won't buy it when my old phone still works.

# B GOAL Talk about Needs and Wants

## Listening

**A** 🎧 32 **Listen to a conversation. Choose the best option.**

1. The speakers are _____ students.

   **a.** high school        **b.** university        **c.** graduate

2. The speakers are in _____.

   **a.** the United Kingdom    **b.** the United States    **c.** India

3. The woman talks about information from a _____.

   **a.** website        **b.** survey        **c.** class

4. The man wishes he had more _____.

   **a.** money to spend        **b.** classes to keep him busy

   **c.** time to spend with friends

**B** 🎧 32 **Listen again and answer the questions.**

1. How does the man feel about his life now?

   _____

2. Who used to do many things for the man?

   _____

3. How does the woman feel about the information she read?

   _____

4. How does the woman feel about the amount of work she is doing?

   _____

5. How does the man feel about the amount of homework he has?

   _____

---

**PRONUNCIATION: Content vs. Function Words**

In sentences, *content words* have specific meaning and receive greater stress. Other words have a grammatical function and receive less stress.

**Content Words**

| Nouns | Main Verbs | Question Words | Adjectives | Adverbs |
|---|---|---|---|---|
| money | speak, buy | why, where, how | wonderful | easily |

**Function Words**

| Pronouns | Auxiliary Verbs | The Verb *Be* | Articles | Prepositions | Conjunctions |
|---|---|---|---|---|---|
| it, she, him | have, is, will, could | is, are, was | the, a, an | in, to, of, at | and, or, but, so |

**C** 🎧 33 **Listen to the stress in each sentence. Then, listen again and repeat.**

1. He <u>wants</u> an <u>active</u> <u>social</u> <u>life</u>.      4. You should <u>think</u> about the <u>future</u>.

2. We <u>have</u> a <u>lot</u> of <u>homework</u>.      5. My <u>family</u> <u>needs</u> the <u>money</u> I <u>make</u>.

3. I'm <u>saving</u> <u>money</u> for a <u>new</u> <u>computer</u>.

**D** Underline the content words. Then practice saying the sentences in pairs.

1. Eating at restaurants is expensive.

2. His life at home was easier.

3. The student from India usually arrives early.

4. Martina wants to buy a new car.

5. My shoes were made in China.

## Communication

**E** Write each item in the appropriate column. Use your own opinion.

| books | clean water | coffee | a computer | flowers | fresh fruit |
| furniture | the internet | money | a phone | public parks | shoes |

| Luxuries | Necessities |
|---|---|
|  |  |
|  |  |
|  |  |
|  |  |

**WORD FOCUS**

**Necessities** are things we need, such as food and shelter. **Luxuries** are things we don't really need, but they can be nice to have.

**F** Compare your chart in **E** with a partner's chart. Talk about why you think people do or don't need the items.

✓ **GOAL CHECK**
## Talk about Needs and Wants

What is something you absolutely need? What luxury item do you want very much? Discuss these questions in pairs.

# C GOAL Discuss What Makes People's Lives Better

## Language Expansion: Irregular Past Participles

**A** Fill in each blank with the best word from the box. Use a dictionary to help you.

| | | | |
|---|---|---|---|
| build – built | find – found | fly – flown | give – given |
| know – known | put – put | send – sent | write – written |

1. Gold and diamonds can be _____ in parts of South Africa.

2. Fresh seafood can be _____ by plane to anywhere in the world.

3. Large amounts of cash are usually not _____ in the mail.

4. Iran is _____ for its beautiful handmade rugs.

5. Wedding invitations are sometimes _____ by hand on special paper.

6. Houses here are _____ for large families, so they usually have several bedrooms.

7. Jewelry is sometimes _____ as a special gift.

8. The glass vases are _____ into special boxes to protect them.

## Grammar

**Children are happy in their primary school in Cahuita, Costa Rica.**

| Passive Voice with *By* | |
|---|---|
| The passive voice is usually used without a *by* phrase. | High-quality cars **are produced** in South Korea. |
| A *by* phrase is used when we want to say who or what does something (the agent). | The cars **are made** <u>by specially trained workers</u>. Each rug **is created** <u>by a different artist</u>, so no two rugs are alike. |

**B** Read the sentences and cross out the unimportant *by* phrases.

1. The Mercedes-Benz is made in Germany ~~by people~~.
2. This necklace was given to me by my grandmother.
3. King Tut's tomb was discovered by Howard Carter.
4. My car was stolen on April 19 ~~by someone~~.
5. The company was started by the new owner's grandfather.
6. Several kinds of fruit are grown in Ontario, Canada ~~by fruit growers~~.

**C** Rewrite each sentence as a question in the passive voice.

1. Children need to be taught good manners.
   Why _____

2. Money should be kept in a bank.
   Why _____

3. Good jobs are often given to people with a good education.
   Why _____

4. Hard work is valued as much as education by some employers.
   Why _____

## Conversation

**D** 🎧 34 Close your book and listen to the conversation. Why is education valuable?

**Lance:** Gary, do you think people's lives are improved by money?

**Gary:** It depends. Some people don't have enough money to buy necessities. Their lives are definitely improved by having more money.

**Lance:** What about other people?

**Gary:** Well, when you have enough money for the basics, I think your life can be improved by education.

**Lance:** Interesting! Is your education improving your life?

**Gary:** Sure. I hope to get a good job someday because of my education.

**Lance:** For me, though, my life would be improved by having a nice car.

**Gary:** OK, but nice cars cost money. So, you need to get a job first.

**SPEAKING STRATEGY**

We use **It depends** to say that something is not always true. Then, we often explain our reasons.

## ✓ GOAL CHECK
### Discuss What Makes People's Lives Better

In pairs, discuss how these things improve your life.

| a big house | electronics | fame | good health | nice clothes |

# D GOAL Talk about Different Lifestyles

## Reading

**A** **MY WORLD** In pairs, discuss the choices. Which would you choose, and why?

- More money or more free time?
- A larger home or traveling more?
- A new car or a cleaner environment?
- Nice things for yourself or for your children?

**B** Discuss the questions in pairs.

1. Look at the title of the article. What do you think it means?
2. Do you think some people live a "zero-waste" lifestyle?

**C** Circle **T** for *true* or **F** for *false*.

1. Kathryn Kellogg and her husband produce 1,500 pounds of trash each year.    T    F
2. Posts on Kellogg's blog encourage people to make better choices.    T    F
3. The Frugalwoods' main goal is to save money.    T    F
4. The Frugalwoods' daughter enjoys being outdoors with her parents.    T    F
5. So far, the zero-waste lifestyle is popular only in the US.    T    F

**D** Discuss the questions in pairs.

1. What are some ways you try to throw away or waste less?
2. Do you think a zero-waste lifestyle is a good goal? Why?
3. Would you and your friends enjoy reading the blogs from the article? Explain.

---

## ✓ GOAL CHECK

Discuss the questions in pairs.

1. What might you like and dislike about a person's lifestyle?
2. What might make a lifestyle satisfying for the person?

> I might like having an important job at a bank.

> I think it might be more satisfying to work outdoors.

# A Zero-Waste Lifestyle

In the United States, throwing away a lot of trash is not unusual. The average American produces around 1,500 pounds, or around 680 kilos, of trash each year. On the other hand, everyone has choices when it comes to their lifestyle, and the US is also home to people like Kathryn Kellogg. She and her husband live in California, and they throw away very little. In fact, the amount of trash they produced in two years—every bit of waste that they could not recycle, reuse, or turn into **compost**—fit into a small glass **jar**.

Kellogg writes a popular **blog** called Going Zero Waste. Her blog posts encourage others to make better choices and live better lives. She reports that she and her husband are saving around $5,000 a year at the grocery store. Instead of buying prepared foods and commercial cleaning products, they buy fresh foods that they cook themselves and make their own cleaning products. They even make their own deodorant and skincare products.

The real goal of going zero waste, however, is not just to save money. For another couple, who call themselves Mr. and Mrs. Frugalwoods, the goal is to enjoy life more and spend more quality time together as a family. Their blog, Frugalwoods, includes articles about buying less and saving money, but also about growing food at their home in Vermont and raising their baby girl. Mrs. Frugalwoods says that their daughter, "...is our mini gardener/hiker who **adores** being outside in nature with her parents every season of the year."

Many people would like to waste less—less money, less plastic, less food—and the internet is full of ideas to help them. A quick search will find stories that include making compost from banana peels, recycling old clothing, and reducing waste while traveling. There are people living zero-waste lifestyles and blogging about it not only in the US, but in many other countries as well. For all of these people, choosing to live a zero-waste lifestyle is about using less and throwing away less, but also about living a happier and more satisfying life.

**compost**  a mixture of decayed plants used to enrich garden soil
**jar**  glass container used for storing food
**blog**  website with a diary or journal about a certain subject
**adores**  loves very much

**Growing one's own vegetables is part of a lifestyle choice.**

# **GOAL** Set Priorities

## Communication

**A** **MY WORLD** What is important in your life right now? In pairs, add three more items to the list.

- spending time with friends

- having new things: clothes, telephone, etc.

- studying and learning new things

- _____

- _____

- _____

**B** Tell your partner which two or three things in **A** are the most important to you. Explain why.

**C** Get together with another pair of students. Share your lists from **A**. Explain the items you added to the list.

**Elias Weiss Friedman enjoys taking photos of dogs for a living.**

## Writing

**D** What are some of the things you want to have in your future life? They could be material or non-material things.

| Things I want |
|---|
| • |
| • |
| • |
| • |
| • |

---

**WRITING SKILL: Using Sequence Words**

When you describe the order of things or the steps in a process, sequence words help the reader understand your ideas.

**Sequence words:** *first, second, finally, before / after___, next, last, once___, then, eventually*

**Example:** When I think about my future, I have some priorities. **First**, I want to get a good education. That will open a lot of doors for me. **Next**, I need to find a job. I plan to work for someone else for a few years and **then** start my own business. **After** that, I might get married and start a family. **Eventually**, I'll retire and let my children run the business.

---

**E** Write a paragraph about your future life. Use the list you made in **D** for ideas. Use sequence words, and use the paragraph in the Writing Skill box as a model.

**F** Tell a partner what you decided to include in your paragraph. Explain why each idea is important to you.

> I decided that saving money for the future is important to me.

> What will the money eventually be used for?

 **GOAL CHECK** Set Priorities

Make a list of priorities for yourself and for your partner. What do you need to do right now? What can you do in the future to help you reach your goals?

> The first priority for both of us should be getting a degree.

> Yes, and after that, I really want to travel for a month.

# VIDEO JOURNAL

# THE DOGIST

**A** Discuss the questions in pairs.

1. Why do some people like to post photos on social media websites?

2. How do you think people feel when other people "like" their posts?

3. Do you enjoy seeing photos of animals online? Why, or why not?

**B** Match each sentence beginning to its ending. You may use a dictionary to help you.

1. ___ When you **pose** for a picture,...

2. ___ If you **hang out** with dogs,...

3. ___ If you **personify** an animal,...

4. ___ When you feel **loneliness**,...

5. ___ If you are **unemployed**,...

6. ___ If you give a dog a **treat**,...

a. you make it seem more like a person.

b. the dog will eat it and be happy.

c. you don't have a job.

d. spending more time with people can help.

e. you get ready for the picture to be taken.

f. you spend time with them.

**C** Watch the video. Circle the correct answer.

1. The photographer takes his photos *indoors* / *outdoors*.

2. The photographer *does* / *does not* have a regular job.

3. The photographer wears equipment to protect his *knees* / *arms*.

4. The photographer takes pictures in *New York* / *Los Angeles*.

5. The photos do not usually include the *dog's* / *owner's* face.

6. The photographer says dogs need food and water / *love* to be happy.

**D** Watch again and answer the questions.

1. Does the photographer ask permission before he takes a dog's picture? _____

2. How does the photographer get dogs to "pose"? _____

3. According to the photographer, why do so many people like his photos?
   _____

4. What information about each dog does the photographer include on the photos?
   _____

5. Why does the photographer say he feels "less lonely" now?
   _____

6. How long has the photographer been "The Dogist"? _____

**E** Read the quotation from "The Dogist." Discuss the questions below in small groups.

"I ask people sometimes, if you had all the money in the world, what would you do? If I had all the money, I would probably travel with my camera and hang out with dogs—I'm doing that."

Elias Weiss Friedman, "The Dogist"

1. Do you think the photographer has a satisfying life? Explain.

2. What would you do if you had a very large amount of money?

3. What other careers might be very enjoyable for the people who do them? Why do you think so?

**F** In your group, talk about things The Dogist needs and doesn't need for his lifestyle.

| | | |
|---|---|---|
| a camera | a computer | his own car |
| his own dog | a large house | to live in a city |
| special clothing | special equipment | your idea ___ |

He needs to have a good camera.

He doesn't need to have a regular job.

99

Gray whale in San Ignacio Lagoon, a part of the Vizcaino Biosphere Reserve, in Mexico

## UNIT 8 GOALS

A. Talk about Consequences

B. Discuss Ways to Solve Future Problems

C. Describe a Situation

D. Discuss Conservation Projects

E. Explain a Conservation Issue

# GOAL Talk about Consequences

## Vocabulary

**A** Look at the picture. What do you know about this animal? Tell a partner.

**B** Read the text.

### Climate Change

Polar bears live on Arctic sea ice. It is their natural habitat. From these ice platforms, they can catch seals to eat. The ice is very important for polar bears, but sadly it is disappearing because of climate change. The world is getting warmer and the Arctic ice is melting. If the ice disappears, polar bears will have a hard time finding food.

If we don't try to stop climate change, polar bears and other wild animals are going to become extinct. We need to protect these endangered species. They are all an important part of the natural world.

**C** Match the words in blue to their meaning. Change the form when necessary.

1. _____protect_____ to keep safe from danger
2. _____ a kind of animal or plant
3. _____ to change from solid to liquid because of heat
4. _____ to stop being seen
5. _____ doesn't exist any more
6. _____ the weather of a place over time
7. _____ the place where an animal usually lives
8. _____ in nature, not controlled by people

**WORD FOCUS**

Species that are near extinction are **endangered species**.

**D** Complete the sentences with a blue word.

1. When people cut down forests, many _____ animals lose their _____.
2. The Arctic has a cold _____. In the winter, the temperature can be –50°C.
3. Some people are trying to _____ nature by changing some of their habits.
4. The number of gorillas in the world now is very small. They are an endangered _____.

A polar bear at the water's edge on Rudolph Island, part of the Franz Josef Land archipelago in Russia

**E** **MY WORLD** In pairs, talk about other endangered animals you know about.

## Grammar

| Real Conditionals in the Future | |
|---|---|
| We use the real conditional for situations that can happen in the future. | If the world **gets hotter**, the arctic ice **will melt**. The arctic ice **will melt if** the world **gets hotter**. |
| Conditional sentences have two parts: the condition and the result. The condition or the result can be first in the sentence. | If the world **gets hotter**, the ice **is going to melt**. The ice **is going to melt if** the world gets hotter. |

**F** Read the text in **B** again and <u>underline</u> the conditional sentences.

**G** Complete the sentences with the correct form of the verbs in parentheses.

1. Polar bears _____ (lose) their habitat if the sea ice _____ (melt).

2. If we _____ (take) action now, we _____ (help) protect nature.

3. If the temperature _____ (get) higher, more wild animals _____ (be) endangered.

4. Polar bears _____ (try) to find food in towns if they _____ (have to) live on land.

5. If humans _____ (not control) climate change, more species _____ (become) extinct.

**H** Discuss these situations in pairs. Write sentences to describe them in your notebook. What will happen if ...

1. the climate continues to change?
2. the polar bears' habitat disappears?
3. polar bears can't catch enough seals?
4. people protect polar bears?
5. polar bears become extinct?
6. polar bears try to find food in towns?

 **GOAL CHECK** Talk about Consequences

Look at the problems in the chart. How will these problems affect nature? Write notes in the consequences column. Then, talk about the problems and their consequences in pairs.

> If climate change continues,...

> More animals will... if...

| Problems | Consequences |
|---|---|
| climate change | |
| pollution | |
| energy use | |

# **GOAL** Discuss Ways to Solve Future Problems

## Listening

1. Atlantic Ocean
2. Pacific Ocean
3. Indian Ocean
4. Mediterranean Sea

**A** Match the names in the box with the places on the map. Write the numbers.

**B** 🎧 36 Listen to the radio program about the bluefin tuna and circle the three places it talks about on the map.

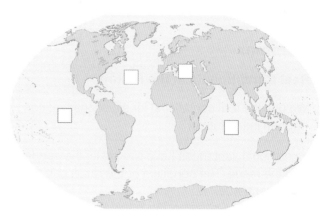

**C** 🎧 37 Listen and fill in the blanks.

**Bluefin Tuna**

1. up to _____ feet long

2. weighs more than _____

3. colors: _____ ,

   _____ , _____

4. swims more than

   _____ miles an hour

5. lives up to

   _____ years

**D** 🎧 38 Listen and complete the sentences.

1. In _____ , people use it to make sushi, and in _____ , people love to cook big pieces for tuna steaks.

2. If the boats _____ big bluefins, there _____ young fish in the future.

3. Only _____ of the original population of bluefins was left.

4. If the big boats _____ the fishing in the Mediterranean, many poor people _____ their work.

5. If this amazing fish _____ , the seas _____ a great treasure.

**Fish farm in Bodrum, Turkey**

**E** **MY WORLD** Discuss these questions in pairs.

1. Is fish cheap or expensive where you live? How often do you eat it?
2. Do you know where the fish you eat comes from?

## Pronunciation: Phrases in sentences

**F** 🎧 39 Listen and repeat the sentences. Notice how they're divided into phrases.

1. A bluefin tuna | can swim very fast | and live a long time.
2. In Japan, | people use it | to make sushi.

**G** 🎧 40 Draw lines to divide these sentences into phrases. Listen and check your answers. Then, practice saying the sentences.

1. If they catch all the big fish, the species won't survive.
2. The bluefin tuna is also delicious.
3. There are international rules for fishing.
4. Bluefin tuna lived in the Pacific Ocean and the Indian Ocean.
5. It is important to try to understand how our actions affect nature.

## Communication

 Read the information. What does *sustainable* mean?

Fish is one of the world's favorite foods. Around the world, the average person eats 36 pounds (16 kg) of fish every year. But many kinds of fish around the world are disappearing because people catch too many of them. Scientists say that 90 percent of the biggest fish are gone now. If we catch too many big fish now, there won't be any baby fish in the future. Some species of fish will become extinct. Our way of fishing now is not **sustainable**—if it continues, it will hurt the environment.

## ✓ GOAL CHECK  Discuss Ways to Solve Future Problems

In groups, discuss ways to solve fishing problems.

1. Read each plan. What will happen if we follow each one? Write some notes.

| **Plan A: Don't eat fish!** Tell people to stop buying and eating fish. Put ads in newspapers and magazines, and make TV commercials to explain why fishing hurts the environment. | **Plan B: Safe fish symbol** Make a special symbol for fish that are caught in a sustainable way. Make commercials to tell people to look for this symbol in supermarkets and restaurants. | **Plan C: Strict laws about fishing** Make stronger laws about how many fish people can catch. Send special police in fast boats to all of the fishing areas to make sure that fishing boats follow the laws. |
|---|---|---|

2. Discuss the plans with your group.
3. As a group, decide which is the best plan.
4. Explain your decision to the class.

# GOAL Describe a Situation

## Language Expansion: Adverbs of Manner

**A** Read the text and answer the question. What does the rescue center do?

The Moholoholo Wildlife Rehabilitation Centre in South Africa works hard to protect local wild animals. This rescue center helps many different species, from lions, leopards, and cheetahs to rhinoceros and eagles. They rescue them from a lot of dangerous situations. Sometimes the animals are badly injured or they have been poisoned, and often they have been orphaned because of poaching. The center looks after the animals carefully. Some animals recover quickly and they can be released into the wild again rapidly, but a few animals have to stay permanently. At the center, they know that conservation is important, so they have an education program, too. People can visit the center to learn about wildlife and protecting the environment.

A critically endangered Northern white rhinoceros at the Dvur Kralove Zoo in Dvur Kralove nad Labem in the Czech Republic

**WORD FOCUS**

If you are **orphaned**, you don't have your parents anymore.

**B** Write the blue words from **A** in the chart.

**Adverbs of Manner**

| | |
|---|---|
| Adverbs of manner tell us *how* an action is done. The adverb usually follows the verb. | Orphaned animals can't survive **easily** without their mothers.<br>They need to help poisoned animals **quickly**. |
| Some adverbs are irregular. | good – well<br>hard – hard |

| Adjective | Adverb of Manner |
|---|---|
| bad | |
| careful | |
| hard | |
| permanent | |
| quick | |
| rapid | |

**C** Complete the sentences with the adverb forms of the adjectives in the box.

| | |
|---|---|
| bad | careful |
| good | happy |
| hard | quiet |
| slow | |

1. The vet checks the animals _____ before they enter the center.

2. The baby cheetah is eating _____ now and it plays _____ with the other cheetah.

3. The visitors watched the baby rhino _____. They didn't want to frighten him.

4. The staff at the center works _____ to help the animals.

5. The lion was walking _____ because its leg was _____ injured.

## Grammar

**Review of Quantifiers**

| With count nouns | | | With non-count nouns | | |
|---|---|---|---|---|---|
| a few | a lot of | animals | a little | a lot of | food |
| many | some | | some | too little | |
| too few | too many | | too much | | |

**D** Write **C** for *count nouns* or **NC** for *non-count nouns*.

Wildlife rescue centers save (1) _____ animals that are in danger. Often, the
animals are sick or hurt, so they need medicine. And of course, they all need
(2) _____ food and (3) _____ water. The staff works hard to take care of them.
The (4) _____ centers help the animals recover so they can go back to their
natural (5) _____ habitat.

**E** Circle the correct quantifier in each sentence.

1. There are *too few* / *too little* visitors to the center. They want more people
   to come.
2. The center spends *many* / *a lot of* money taking care of the animals.
3. They took *a few* / *a little* lions back to the wild yesterday.
4. Hunters kill *too many* / *too much* leopards.

**F** **MY WORLD** What animals do rescue centers near you help? Discuss in pairs.

## Conversation

**G** 🎧 41 Listen to the conversation with your book closed. Why was the deer at the
rescue center?

**SPEAKING STRATEGY**

Look at the questions
Dan asks. We use
questions to keep a
conversation going.

**Dan:** I didn't know you worked at the wildlife rescue center.

**Carmen:** I'm really interested in conservation, so I started helping there last
year. It's hard work, but I see some amazing animals. The vet brought
in a beautiful deer this morning. It was badly injured.

**Dan:** Oh no, what happened to it?

**Carmen:** A car hit it on the highway last night.

**Dan:** So, what did you do?

**Carmen:** Well, the vet checked the deer carefully, and she found it has a
broken leg.

**Dan:** If she recovers quickly, will she go back to the wild?

**Carmen:** We hope so.

 **GOAL CHECK** Describe a Situation

Describe one of the situations in the box to a partner.
Use adverbs of manner and quantifiers.

| wild animal hunting | poaching | circus animals |
|---|---|---|
| destruction of animals' habitats | | |

# D

## GOAL Discuss Conservation Projects

### Reading

**A** Look at the photo. What do you think the article will tell you? Write your ideas.

_____

**B** What do you think *overfishing* means? Discuss in pairs.

**C** Read the article and circle the main idea.

| | |
|---|---|
| Change is possible. | Straws can kill turtles. |
| Trash is the ocean's main problem. | We need to protect the oceans. |

**D** Read the article again. Answer the questions.

1. What was happening in Madagascar?

2. How have they solved the problem?

3. What do you think Samson means when he says, "We are all in this together"?

4. Why are straws a problem for the environment?

5. What has happened as a result of the Sea Turtle Conservancy's project in Florida?

### ✓ GOAL CHECK

1. What can you do to make a difference for the environment? Write a list of specific actions and habits you could change.

2. Share your list in pairs. Do you have any ideas that are the same? What different ideas do you have?

3. Discuss a conservation project.

   **a.** Write a list of local or national conservation projects that you know about.

   **b.** Share your list in pairs. Discuss the different projects.

   **c.** Join another pair. Choose one of the projects to research and find out more about it.

   **d.** With your group, present the project you researched to the class.

# Making a Difference: Small Changes

Human actions are affecting the environment, and if we don't try to change things, we will lose more and more of the natural world. Even though it is hard, we can make a difference. Each small change is important, and luckily more individuals and **organizations** around the world are becoming involved in conservation projects.

In Madagascar, a fisherman named Samson has become a voice for the ocean and is helping his **community** take better care of its local waters. He and the other fishermen realized that they were catching fewer and fewer fish every day. They were overfishing. Working with the World Wide Fund for Nature (WWF), Samson learned that they had to fish more carefully. He realized that they shouldn't catch so many young fish because if there

are too few of them in the ocean, there won't be enough adult fish to reproduce. Samson now works with his community to help fishermen change their techniques so that fishing can be sustainable. He believes that protecting the ocean is everybody's job. As he says, "Take your responsibilities with courage and never think that you are alone. We are all in this together."

On the other side of the world, in Florida, in the US, the Sea Turtle Conservancy (STC) organization noticed that there were always a lot of single-use plastic items, like coffee stirrers, bottles, and drinking straws, on the beaches. All of these items can hurt the ocean wildlife terribly. Straws are especially dangerous for turtles because they can get **stuck** in turtles' noses and hurt them very badly. So, the STC started the project "Where are the straws?" asking local restaurants to stop giving customers straws with their drinks. Now, many restaurants will only give straws if customers ask for them, and the straws

they do give out are paper, not plastic. If we don't use plastic straws (or other single-use plastic items), there will be less plastic pollution in the oceans. Not using plastic straws is just one way each of us can **contribute to** protecting ocean wildlife.

Those are just two of the many conservation efforts found all over the world today. Mexico, for example, has successful projects for sea turtle protection similar to that of Florida, and Costa Rica has its own very effective ocean conservation initiatives. These projects all show us that change is possible and that it can start with small actions in our own community. We are part of the problem. It's time to be part of the solution.

**organization** a group of people who work together
**community** a group of people who live in the same area
**stuck** if something is stuck, it can't move
**contribute to** to help or give support to something

An endangered green sea turtle entangled in a fishing net swimming underwater

**GOAL** Explain a Conservation Issue

## Communication

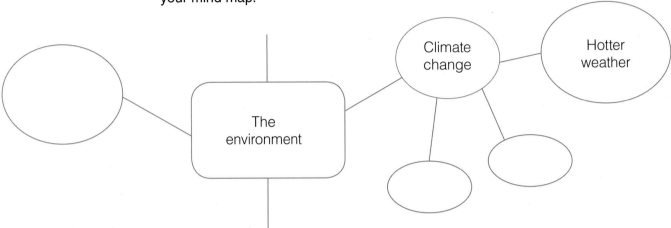

A Draw a mind map in your notebook. In the center, write *the environment*. Brainstorm problems related to the environment in your country. Write them in your mind map.

B Share your mind map in pairs. Explain the problems you wrote.

Chonin, a silverback mountain gorilla, in Parc des Volcans, Rwanda.

**C** In pairs, identify the causes and consequences of each problem and add them to your mind map. Then, join another pair and discuss possible solutions for the problems. What can local people do? What actions will help solve the problem or improve the situation?

> If people use their cars less, climate change will be slower.

> Yes, that's true. We can make a carpool plan at work so fewer people drive to work every day.

## Writing

**D** Complete the sentences about a problem in nature in your country.

1. If we believe in conservation, we will _____.

2. If _____, many animals will be saved.

3. If people want to make positive changes, they will _____.

**E** Write *but, so,* and *even though* in the correct places in the paragraph.

By the 1990s, many species of animals were endangered in Namibia because of poaching. The situation was serious, (1) _____ conservationists needed to find a way to protect the animals. They found one, (2) _____ it wasn't what you would expect: they asked poachers for help. (3) _____ this seemed crazy, I think it was a great idea. If we want to protect endangered species, we need to consider every solution.

**WRITING STRATEGY**

Conjunctions are used to connect ideas within sentences.

**F** In your notebook, write a paragraph explaining an environmental issue in your country. Use the paragraph in **E** to help you. Explain the causes and consequences of the problem and give some possible solutions.

**G** In pairs, exchange paragraphs. How can your partner improve his or her paragraph? Use your partner's comments to make corrections to your paragraph.

## ✓ GOAL CHECK Explain a conservation issue

In small groups, share your paragraphs from **G**. Choose one of the issues to explain to the class.

# VIDEO JOURNAL

# TED TALKS

# LIFE LESSONS FROM BIG CATS

## BEFORE YOU WATCH

**A** In pairs, look at the picture and answer the questions.

1. What kind of animal is in the photo?
2. Where do these animals live?
3. What else do you know about these animals and their habitat?

**B** Look at the words in the box. Complete the paragraph with the correct words. Not all words will be used.

> **collectively** shared or done by a group of people
> **condone** to allow (something that may be considered wrong) to continue
> **crash** to go down very suddenly and quickly
> **disrupt** to cause (something) to be unable to continue in the normal way
> **pride** a group of lions
> **revenue stream** a flow of money that is made by or paid to a business or an organization

Africa's big cats are endangered, and we are all (1) _____ responsible. Soon, the (2) _____ of lions may disappear. Because we (3) _____ hunting and other activities that put them at risk, their numbers have (4) _____ in the last 50 years. And it's not only the big cats that are in danger—ecotourism brings in a large (5) _____ to Africa. If the cats disappear, so will the money and jobs.

## WHILE YOU WATCH

**C** Watch the TED Talk. Circle the main idea.

1. It's necessary to study big cats over many years.
2. If the big cats disappear, many other species may disappear.
3. Beverly and Dereck Joubert believe that big cats are beautiful.

## AFTER YOU WATCH

**D** Match the phrases to the information from the video.

1. number of lions alive now _____
2. number of leopards left in the wild _____
3. years the Jouberts have been filming big cats _____
4. amount of ecotourism revenue stream _____
5. number of years the Jouberts followed Legadema _____

   a. $80 billion
   b. 5
   c. 20,000
   d. 50,000
   e. 28

**E** Complete the summary with the words in the box.

> extinction   passionate   photographing
> respect   survive

Beverly and Dereck Joubert are (1) _____ about protecting the African wilderness. They have spent many years studying and (2) _____ big cats. In the last 50 years, these cats have been pushed to the edge of (3) _____ by hunters. The Jouberts believe that if the big cats are viewed with (4) _____, they can survive. And if the big cats (5) _____, they can help us maintain our connection to nature and to other human beings.

**BEVERLY AND DERECK JOUBERT**

Documentary Filmmakers /
Conservationists, National Geographic
Explorers-in-Residence

Beverly and Dereck Joubert's **idea worth spreading** is
that big cats like lions and leopards have big personalities
and getting to know them can help protect Africa. Watch
the Jouberts' full TED Talk on TED.com.

# Life Now and in the Past

A visitor at the
12th-century Bayon
Temple in Angkor,
Cambodia

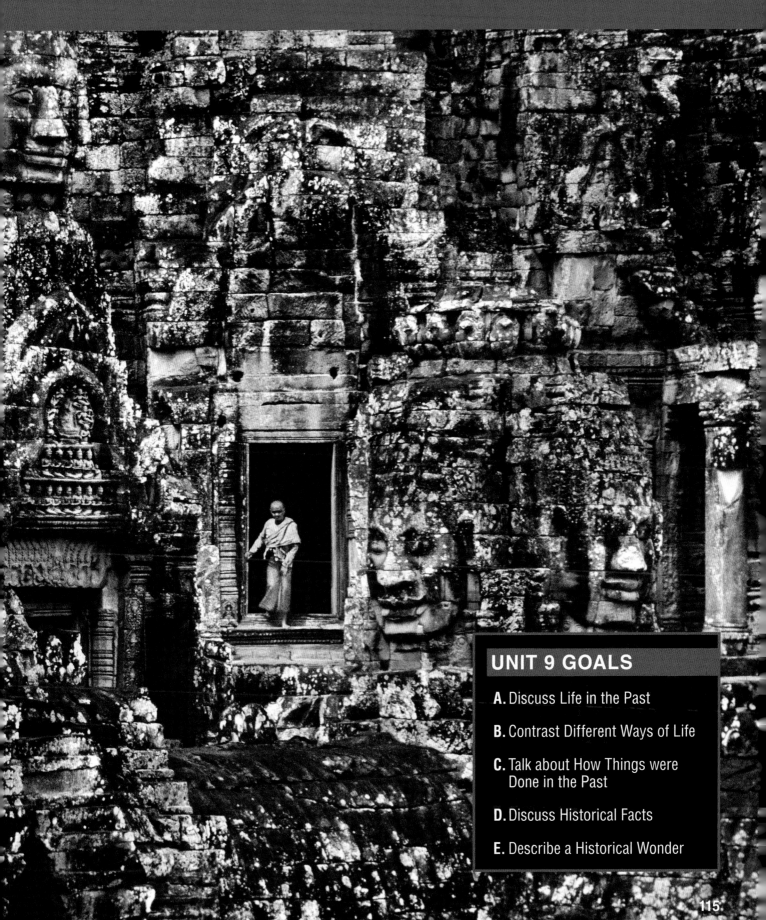

**Look at the photo and answer the questions:**

**1** What do you see in the photo?

**2** What ancient places exist where you live?

## UNIT 9 GOALS

**A.** Discuss Life in the Past

**B.** Contrast Different Ways of Life

**C.** Talk about How Things were Done in the Past

**D.** Discuss Historical Facts

**E.** Describe a Historical Wonder

115

**GOAL** Discuss Life in the Past

### Vocabulary

**A** Look at the picture. Answer the questions in pairs.

1. What do you know about Marco Polo?

2. Where did he travel? How do you think he traveled?

**B** Read the text.

**Marco Polo
Mosaic from
Palazzo Tursi in
Genoa, Italy**

Today, many people travel from one country to another easily, and even from one continent to another, but long-distance travel used to be very challenging. But even though it was difficult hundreds of years ago, there were always people who wanted to discover new places. Explorers used to travel by land and sea on trips that often took many years, and the result was an exchange of knowledge and culture that changed the world.

Marco Polo (1254–1324) was one of these great explorers. We do not know exactly when or where Polo was born, but he lived in Venice and Genoa, in what is now Italy. In 1271, when he was about 17, he set off on a trip with his father and uncle. They left Italy and traveled east—far beyond the borders of Europe, into Asia.

Marco's father was a merchant searching for opportunities for trade with China. They traveled first by ship, then by horse and camel, through many countries. Everything was very different: they saw amazing places and learned new things. In China, for example, they were surprised to see paper money, eyeglasses, the compass, and silk making.

Marco Polo returned to Italy 24 years later with lots of experiences to share. But he only became famous after his book, *The Description of the World*, was published. The book inspired other world travelers centuries later.

**C** Write each word in blue next to the correct definition or synonym.

1. _____ start a journey
2. _____ giving and receiving
3. _____ difficult
4. _____ buying and selling
5. _____ printed and sold
6. _____ further than
7. _____ a very soft cloth
8. _____ chances

**D** Complete the sentences with the correct form of a blue word.

1. Traveling is an _____ to get to know other people and cultures.

2. We use _____ to make beautiful dresses and shirts.

3. Marco Polo _____ for China in 1271.

4. Living in a foreign country can be very _____ at first.

5. Today, there is a lot of _____ between China and Europe.

## Grammar

| Used to | |
|---|---|
| We use *used to* + base form of a verb to contrast the past with the present. | Long-distance travel **used to be** challenging; now it is easier. Trade between countries **used to take** more time. |
| In questions and negative statements, use *did* / *didn't* + *use to*. | **Did** explorers **use to** travel by horse a lot? How **did** people **use to** travel? People **didn't use to** pay for things with paper money. |

**E** Write questions using the words provided and the correct form of *used to*. Ask a partner your questions.

1. people / travel *How did people use to travel?*

2. trade / take longer _____

3. clothes / people / wear _____

4. merchants / trade _____

**F** 🎧 43 Complete the conversation. Then, listen and check your answers.

> didn't   travel   use   used   used to

**Sue:** Why did people (1) _____ to travel by horse?

**Aki:** Well, there (2) _____ use to be other transportation.

**Sue:** OK, but did everyone use to (3) _____ that way?

**Aki:** No, in some parts of the world they (4) _____ use camels, not horses. Why are you so interested in how people (5) _____ to travel?

**Sue:** I'm writing about transportation in the past for my history class.

**G** **MY WORLD** Make a list of things that were different 100 years ago where you live.

---

 **GOAL CHECK** Discuss Life in the Past

1. Complete the chart.

| | Before | Now |
|---|---|---|
| transportation | *horses pulled vehicles* | *motor vehicles* |
| communication | | |
| trade | | |
| home life | | |
| education | | |

> People used to travel by sea more. Now we fly to different countries.

> That's right. Travel used to take longer.

2. In pairs, describe what people used to do in the past. Use the topics in the chart and your own ideas.

# **GOAL** Contrast Different Ways of Life

## Listening

**A** Look at the photo. Would you like to live there? Discuss in pairs.

**B** How do you think people used to live in this part of the world 1,000 years ago? Check (✓) the things you think people did.

1. _____ ate fish from the Arctic Ocean
2. _____ lived on small farms
3. _____ followed groups of animals, such as reindeer
4. _____ lived in houses made of wood
5. _____ had their own language and customs

**C** 🎧 44 Listen to a talk about the Sami people and choose the main idea.

**a.** The Sami people depend on animals, especially reindeer, to make a living.

**b.** Life is changing for the Sami people, but some of them still live in traditional ways.

**c.** Many young Sami people want to attend a university and choose a career.

**WORD FOCUS**

Some animal words don't have plural forms:

**bison**     **deer**
**reindeer**    **sheep**

**D** 🎧 44 Listen again and circle **T** for *true* or **F** for *false*. Correct the false sentences to make them true.

1. Traditionally, the Sami people stayed and lived in one place.    **T**   **F**
2. Reindeer were used by the Sami people for food and clothing.    **T**   **F**
3. Most Sami people still live in the traditional way.    **T**   **F**
4. Some Sami people now raise reindeer on farms.    **T**   **F**
5. New laws affect the way Sami people may use land.    **T**   **F**

**E** Do you think it's important to maintain traditions from the past? Or do you think people should focus on the future? Discuss your ideas in pairs.

Sami reindeer herder in the forest in Lapland, Sweden

## Pronunciation

**Reduction of *used to***

When we speak quickly, *used to* is sometimes pronounced /'jus·tə/.

**F** 🎧 45  You will hear each sentence twice. Listen to the full form and the reduced form of *used to*. Listen again and repeat the sentences.

1. The Sami people used to follow their herds of reindeer.
2. They used to sleep in tents.
3. They used to make the tents from reindeer skins.
4. Did the Sami use to raise sheep?
5. No, they didn't use to raise sheep, only reindeer.

**G** Complete the sentences with your own information. Then, share your ideas in pairs. Use the reduced form /'jus·tə/.

1. When I was younger, I used to _____.
2. As a child, I used to want money for _____.
3. In my country, people used to _____.
4. Before I was born, my grandparents used to _____.
5. As children, my parents used to _____.

## Communication

**H** **MY WORLD** How has your culture changed? Write notes to answer the questions below.

1. Fifty years ago in your culture:
   - How old were men and women when they got married?
   - How many children did they use to have?
   - Where did people use to live?
   - What kind of jobs did people use to do?
2. How have these things changed?

WORD FOCUS

**Culture** refers to the way of life, including the general customs and traditions, of a particular group of people.

✓ **GOAL CHECK** Contrast Different Ways of Life

| education | food | housing | language | location | traditions | transportation |

1. How is your way of life different from other cultures you know about?
2. In small groups, discuss your answers. Use the ideas in the box and your own ideas.

## Language Expansion: Separable Phrasal Verbs

bring back
bring up
figure out
help out
put on
turn on

**A** Complete the paragraph with the separable phrasal verb closest in meaning to the verb in parentheses.

Hi, my name is Susie, and I live in the Nunavut Territory in Canada. Life in Nunavut hasn't changed as much as it has in other places. It's true that nowadays we can (1)_____ (start) the furnace when it gets cold instead of building a fire, but we haven't given up our traditional culture. We still (2)_____ (raise) our children in the land our people have lived on for thousands of years. We teach them to (3)_____ (wear) our traditional clothing to stay warm in the winter. When they're old enough, we teach them to (4)_____ (discover, solve) solutions to everyday problems. We teach them to (5)_____ (return) anything they borrow. And most importantly, we teach them to always (6)_____ (aid) their family and their community. Those things will never change.

**B** Answer the questions. Use pronouns and the separable phrasal verbs in **A**.

1. What do you do with children? _____
2. What do you do with shoes? _____
3. How do you assist your friends? _____
4. How do you understand something? _____
5. What do you do with a borrowed book? _____
6. What do you do to the heat when it's cold? _____

**Inuit man fishing through hole in ice near Arviat, in Hudson Bay, Canada**

## Grammar

| Passive Voice in the Past | |
|---|---|
| Use the active voice in the past to focus on the subject of a sentence. | Parents **raised** their children differently in the past. |
| Use the passive voice in the past to focus on the object or receiver of a past action. | Children **were raised** differently in the past (by their parents). |
| Form the past passive with *was* or *were* + the past participle of a verb. | My father **was taught** to always help other people. |

**C** Match the sentence parts. In your notebook, write complete sentences with the past passive form of a verb from the box.

1. Paper money _____
2. Explorers _____
3. The Sami tents _____
4. Fires _____
5. Reindeer _____

a. from reindeer skin.
b. in China.
c. by the Sami people.
d. when it was cold.
e. by Marco Polo's stories.

build
herd
inspire
invent
make

## Conversation

**D**  **46** Listen to the conversation with your book closed. Why is Luisa interested in mail delivery in the past?

**Luisa:** Hi, Carl. Can I ask you a question?

**Carl:** Sure. Go ahead.

**Luisa:** What do you know about how mail used to be delivered?

**Carl:** Do you mean letters and packages? Well, I guess they were taken on horseback to places in the same country, and by ship to other countries.

**Luisa:** Right, so it used to take a really long time.

**Carl:** Oh yes! When the telegram was invented in the 1800s, people were finally able to send messages quickly.

**Luisa:** Then, in the 20th century, when the internet was developed, everything changed in communication!

**Carl:** Definitely! But why are you asking me about mail delivery?

**Luisa:** I'm giving a presentation in my history class on how communication has changed over the years. I was just practicing for it!

**Carl:** Well I hope I helped! Good luck!

**Luisa:** Thanks, Carl!

**SPEAKING STRATEGY**

Notice Carl's question: *Do you mean letters and packages?* This is a clarification question. We ask clarification questions to make sure we have understood something correctly.

✔ **GOAL CHECK** Talk about How Things Were Done in the Past

1. Look at the timeline. How has public education changed? Discuss in pairs. Use *used to.*

**Public education**

→

300 years ago:
Girls weren't allowed to learn to read.
Many students left school at age 12.

50 years ago:
Girls were allowed to go to school.
Boys and girls were taught mostly different things.

Now:
Girls and boys learn the same things.
Students study until age 18.

2. How were the topics in the box done before public services were developed, and how are they done now? Choose one and draw a timeline.

| garbage collection | health care | public transportation | water |

## **GOAL** Discuss Historical Facts

### Reading

**A** Have you heard of the Silk Road? Tell your partner anything you know about it or what you think it is.

**B** Scan the article and find these numbers. What do they refer to?

1453 _____

4,000 _____

13 _____

14 _____

**C** Read the article. Circle **T** for *true* or **F** for *false*.

1. Marco Polo named the Silk Routes.          **T  F**

2. The routes were only dangerous in the
13th century.                                **T  F**

3. Silk was the most famous item that
came from China.                             **T  F**

4. Diseases traveled along the Silk Routes.  **T  F**

5. Samarkand is the only World Heritage
site along the Silk Routes.                  **T  F**

**D** Answer the questions.

1. Why were the routes dangerous for merchants?

   _____

2. Why is Marco Polo important?

   _____

3. Which goods influenced western culture the most?

   _____

4. How were cultural elements such as art and
scientific knowledge exchanged?

   _____

5. Why do tourists visit the Silk Routes today?

   _____

### ✓ GOAL CHECK

1. In pairs, discuss how the Silk Routes have
influenced modern life.

2. Think of an event or development in your
country from the past. Write notes about it. In
small groups, share your information.

# The Silk Routes

Most of us have heard of the Silk Road, and we probably imagine one long road that made its way from Europe to China, providing opportunities for trade between the West and the East centuries ago. However, it was actually a **network** of roads, or routes. Marco Polo described these routes in the book that was published about his travels, but he didn't give them the name we use today; a 19th-century German traveler, Ferdinand von Richthofen, began using the terms *Seidenstrasse* (silk route) and *Seidenstrassen* (silk routes).

The Silk Routes were used regularly by merchants in caravans of horses and camels between 130 **BCE** and 1453 CE, but traveling along them was challenging. The routes ran 6,400 kilometers (4,000 miles) from China all the way to western Europe and passed through many different countries and types of geography, including mountains and deserts. There was also the **risk** of meeting robbers on the way. But even though there were dangers, many **goods** were transported in both directions.

The routes were safest during the 13th century, when Genghis Khan's Mongol Empire controlled them. Genghis Khan was a strong Mongolian soldier and leader. He created a unified Mongolia and a huge empire all the way across Asia. Thanks to Khan, the Silk Routes became safer. Years later, under the rule of Khan's grandson, Kublai Khan, Marco Polo was able to make his famous journey.

From Polo's writings, we know of some of the goods merchants traded from country to country. Chinese silk is obviously the most well known and gives the road its name, but there were many more. From East to West, trade included tea, spices, rice, paper, and gunpowder, among others. From West to East, some examples are horses, honey, the grapevine, glass, and animal furs.

The exchange of goods was of course very important, and the arrival in the West of paper, gunpowder, and spices, in particular, had a huge influence on life there. But beyond goods, the Silk Routes were also responsible for the exchange and sharing of forms of culture between all of the civilizations along the routes. Art, religion, philosophy, and language, as well as knowledge of science, architecture, and technology, were exchanged as travelers and merchants made their trips through the different countries. The exchange wasn't all positive, however. It's possible, for example, that the Black Death **plague** in Europe in the 14th century was carried from Asia to the West along the Silk Routes.

Nowadays, goods are transported around the world by planes, trains, and ships, but the Silk Road has not been lost. Along the routes, there are many *UNESCO World Heritage sites, such as the beautiful town of Samarkand, Uzbekistan, which is described as a crossroads of cultures. Today, travelers from around the world take tours to different places along the routes to visit these sites and to experience the different cultures along the Silk Road.

*United Nations Educational, Scientific and Cultural Organization

**network** a group formed from parts that are connected together
**BCE** Before Common Era; used when referring to a year before the birth of Jesus Christ
**risk** the possibility of something bad happening
**goods** items for sale (note: always plural)
**plague** a serious disease that kills many people

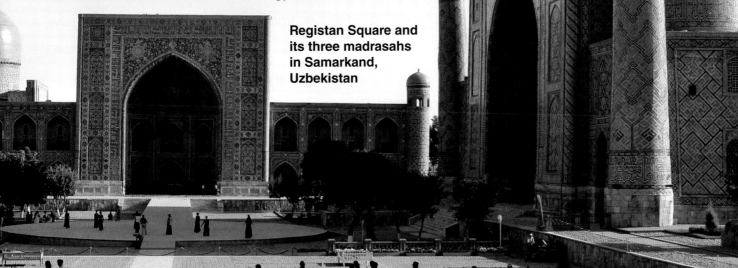

**Registan Square and its three madrasahs in Samarkand, Uzbekistan**

**GOAL** Describe a Historical Wonder

## Communication

A What is a historical wonder? What historical wonders of the world do you know of? Write a list.

B Which words describe your reaction to historical wonders? Discuss in pairs. Explain your choices and add another word of your own.

> amazed   inspired   interested   proud   shocked   your idea _____

C What amazing things did people create in the past? Think of a historical wonder in your country. Write notes about it. What is it like? When was it built? Why? How does it make you feel when you see it?

D Tell a partner about your wonder.

> There is a beautiful, old temple in my town. It was built in...

> What is special about it?

## Writing

E Read the information about the New 7 Wonders of the World.

What does it mean to be a wonder of the world? Both the Seven Wonders of the Ancient World and the New 7 Wonders are examples of humankind's greatest achievements. They are historical sites that show the incredible things we are capable of creating. Of the original Seven Wonders, only the Great Pyramid in Giza, Egypt, still exists, so Swiss-Canadian filmmaker and adventurer, Bernard Weber, started the New 7 Wonders of the World project. He wanted the achievements of the last 2,000 years to be recognized now and remembered in the future. And he wanted the people of the world to decide these new wonders, so he used the internet and telephones for voting. The project began in the year 2000 and the results were announced in 2007. The new wonders include the Great Wall of China, the Colosseum in Rome, and the Taj Mahal in India.

F Complete the description with adjectives from the box.

> amazed   amazing   ancient   famous   huge   interested   stronger

The Great Wall of China was voted one of the New 7 Wonders of the World, and it is also a UNESCO World Heritage Site. It is really (1) _____—some parts were built in the 3rd century BCE—and it is (2) _____—it is more than 20,000 kilometers (12,430 miles) long. Architecturally, it is an (3) _____ construction. The Chinese built the wall over the centuries to protect their country. At the beginning of the 13th century, China was attacked by Genghis Khan's army, because Khan wanted China to be part of the Mongol Empire. His grandson, Kublai Khan, finally achieved this in 1276. Because of historic events like this, China continued to make the wall (4) _____ and better up to the 17th century. It is now one of the world's most (5) _____ landmarks. I was very (6) _____ to read about the Wall's history and I was (7) _____ when I saw it.

 **G** Use the internet to research one of the New 7 Wonders historical sites. Write notes.

 **H** In your notebook, write a description of the site. Use your own words, including adjectives, to describe your reaction to the site. Use the paragraph in **F** to help you.

**WRITING STRATEGY**

Using descriptive adjectives makes your writing more interesting.

✓ **GOAL CHECK** Describe a Historical Wonder

1. Share your description with a partner. Talk about the information that is interesting or surprising to you.

2. How can your partner improve the description? Use your partner's comments to make corrections and improvements.

3. In small groups, share your descriptions of the New 7 Wonders of the World.

**The Colosseum, also known as the Flavian Amphitheater, in Rome, Italy**

# VIDEO JOURNAL

# SEARCHING FOR GENGHIS KHAN

**A** Discuss the questions with a partner.

1. Who was Genghis Khan?

2. Where was he from, and why is he famous?

3. Where do people think Genghis Khan is buried?

4. How is Albert Lin going to find his tomb?

**B** Complete the sentences with the words in the box.

cutting-edge    Forbidden    sacred    sensors

1. Albert Lin is using the most advanced, or _____, technology to find Genghis Khan's tomb.

2. Genghis Khan was buried in a part of Mongolia that is called the _____ Zone, where very few outsiders visit.

3. Because many Mongolians believe Khan's tomb is _____, or holy, Lin and his team can't dig there.

4. Instead, they are using _____, which detect heat, light, sound, and motion.

C Match the words to their definitions.

1. nomadic _____    a. a person who fights and is known for having courage and skill

2. tribe _____    b. moving from place to place

3. warrior _____    c. people with the same language, customs, and beliefs

D Watch the video and check your answers in A, B, and C. Then, circle T for *true* or F for *false*.

1. Albert Lin and his team are working only from the United States to find Genghis's tomb.      T   F

2. Lin always planned to be an explorer.      T   F

3. Lin wants to dig up Genghis's tomb and remove the treasure inside.      T   F

4. Many non-scientists are helping with the research by examining satellite images.      T   F

E Watch the video again. Complete the ideas.

1. Genghis Khan was a warrior and leader in the _____ century.

2. He unified _____ and _____ an empire that stretched across a continent.

3. Lin is a researcher, an _____, and a National Geographic _____.

4. His career is _____.

5. Lin's personal connection to Mongolia is _____.

6. _____ of people looked at _____ images to help Lin find Genghis Khan's tomb.

F **MY WORLD** Lin calls the people around the world who helped him "citizen scientists." Would you like to be a "citizen scientist"? Why? Tell a partner.

G Make predictions, in pairs, about how new technology can be used in exploration and research. Think about exploration on land, under the sea, and in space.

**Albert Lin riding a horse in Mongolia.**

Road to El Chaltén, Los Glaciares
National Park, Santa Cruz, Argentina

**Look at the photo and answer the questions:**

**1** What do you see in this picture?

**2** How would you get to the national park?

## UNIT 10 GOALS

**A.** Talk about Organizing a Trip

**B.** Talk about Different Kinds of Vacations

**C.** Use English at the Airport

**D.** Discuss Travel

**E.** Describe a Cultural Event

# **GOAL** Talk about Organizing a Trip

## Vocabulary

The internet has made organizing a trip a lot easier; you don't need to go to a travel agent anymore. You can do it all yourself with online booking! So, find a travel website and follow these steps:

1. Choose your destination. Where do you want to travel to?

2. Book a flight. Choose your departure and return dates, and then click *search*! If you like the price, click *pay*!

3. Need somewhere to stay? You can make a reservation for a hotel online, too. Set your check-in and check-out dates, and choose the type of room you need.

4. Need travel documents? You can even apply for a visa for some countries online.

**A** Read the text. Then complete the sentences with a blue word or phrase.

1. When you _____, you look for something.

2. You _____ to get permission to enter a country.

3. The date you start your trip is your _____ date.

4. _____ is when you leave the hotel you are staying at.

5. The place you travel to is your _____.

6. With _____, you can buy plane tickets and find a place to stay on the internet.

7. When you buy a plane ticket, you _____.

8. When you _____, you don't pay for the service yet.

**B** Complete each collocation with a blue word from the text above.

1. _____ a hotel      3. _____ time

2. _____ for a passport      4. _____ a tour

5. _____ for

## Grammar

| **Expressing Necessity** | |
|---|---|
| Use *must* + verb to say that something is an obligation or a rule. | Travelers **must apply** for a passport at least six weeks in advance. |
| Use *have to* or *need to* + verb to say that something is necessary. | We **have to book** our flights soon.<br>She **needs to make** a hotel reservation. |
| Use *don't have to* or *don't need to* + verb to say that something is not necessary. | She **doesn't have to get** a visa for Canada.<br>We **don't need to make** a reservation. |

**C** Complete the sentences with *must*, *have to*, *need to*, *don't have to*, or *don't need to*.

1. Airline rules say that passengers _____ be at the gate 15 minutes before departure.

2. We _____ book the tour. It's not a busy time.

3. Passengers _____ be seated during takeoff and landing.

4. If we don't want to pay extra, we _____ leave the hotel before the check-out time.

5. I _____ pack my bag tonight. I leave tomorrow.

6. You _____ make reservations for the train. You can buy the ticket the day you travel.

**D** 🎧 48 Complete the conversation. Then, listen to check your answers.

**Ed:** So, Peter, are you and Maya ready for our trip?

**Peter:** We will be! But first Maya (1) _____ get a new passport, and I (2) _____ apply for the visa.

**Ed:** You need to get started! You (3) _____ go to the embassy for the visa. You can get it online. I booked our hotel online, too. It's so much easier!

**Peter:** OK, thanks for the tip!

You usually need to make a reservation to do extreme activities.

✓ **GOAL CHECK** Talk about Organizing a Trip

Look at the destinations in the box. Add one of your own. Then choose a destination, and complete the chart in your notebook. Finally, talk to a partner about preparing for your trip.

| Canada | Italy | New Zealand | Peru | Thailand _____ |

| Where are you going? | Do you have a passport? | Do you need a visa? (embassy or online) | Tickets (plane, train, bus) | Hotel reservation | Tour | Other |
| --- | --- | --- | --- | --- | --- | --- |
| | | | | | | |

Are you ready for your trip?

Well, I booked my flight to … but I still have to …

How about you? Where are you going on vacation?

# B GOAL Talk about Different Kinds of Vacations

## Listening

**A** Look at the picture. How does it make you feel?

**B** Read the information. What kinds of vacations do you like? Tell a partner.

| 1. Adventure vacation | 2. Relaxing vacation | 3. Learning vacation |
|---|---|---|
| Try exciting sports, like hiking, rafting, or scuba diving. Have amazing experiences to tell your friends about. | Go to a beautiful place to rest and relax. Sleep late, read, listen to music, and enjoy the scenery. | Learn to do something new, like art or music, or take a class in a subject that interests you. |

**C** 🎧 49 Listen to three people talking about their vacations. Which country is each person going to?

**Carla:** _____

**Marcus:** _____

**Julie:** _____

**D** 🎧 49 Listen again and complete the chart.

| | What kind of vacation are they going to have? | What activities are they going to do? |
|---|---|---|
| Carla | | |
| Marcus | | |
| Julie | | |

A longtail boat near the Phi Phi Islands, Thailand

**E** **MY WORLD** Tell a partner about a recent vacation or a vacation you want to go on.

---

**PRONUNCIATION:** Reduction of *have to* and *has to*

When we speak quickly, *have to* and *has to* are pronounced /hæ-ftə/ and /hæ-stə/.

---

**F** 🎧 50 Listen to the sentences. Then practice saying them in pairs.

1. I have to apply for a passport.
2. We have to book our flights.
3. Rosa has to pack her suitcase.
4. They have to check in at six o'clock.
5. Juan has to check his hotel reservation.
6. Do you have to book the tour in advance?

## Communication

**Mexican Traditional Cooking:** Learn to cook delicious, traditional dishes in Oaxaca, Mexico. You will prepare the classic *mole*, with its 34 ingredients, including chocolate and six different types of chili!

**Costa Rican Kayaking:** Have an adventure in Costa Rica. You will go kayaking, hiking, and rafting in the incredible rainforest. Look out for the amazing wildlife, too!

**Beach in Thailand:** Stay in a relaxing beach house on Railay Beach, Thailand! Swim, swing in a hammock, or just do nothing. You don't even have to cook—a chef will prepare all of your meals!

**G** In pairs, talk about the three trips and choose which one you will take together.

> If we go to Thailand, we'll see beautiful beaches!!

**H** What do you have to do before this trip? Think of five things.

> I'll take sunscreen.

**I** What will you take with you? List 10 things.

## ✓ GOAL CHECK
### Talk about Different Kinds of Vacations

Join another pair and talk about your vacation plans. Explain why you chose your vacation and why you did not choose the other destinations. Say what you have to do to prepare for it.

> We didn't choose the beach house because…

> We really like… so we chose…

## C  GOAL  Use English at the Airport

### Language Expansion: At the Airport

A  Write the words from the box next to their meanings.

airline agent
baggage claim
boarding pass
carry-on bag
(online) check-in
gate
security check
terminal

1. _____ registering for your flight at the airport or electronically

2. _____ the person who helps you register for your flight and takes your large bags

3. _____ where travelers arrive and leave from at an airport

4. _____ This has your flight details and seat number. You need it to get on the plane.

5. _____ where you pick up your suitcase after your flight

6. _____ where your bags are checked by security officers

7. _____ the door where you get on the plane

8. _____ a small bag you can take on the plane with you

**REAL LANGUAGE**

You have to **check large bags**. Your **checked baggage** goes in a separate part of the plane and you get it at baggage claim.

B  Complete the paragraph with words from **A**.

When you get to the airport, the first thing you have to do is go to the right (1) _____. Then, you need to find the (2) _____ desk where an (3) _____ will help you. They will check your passport and give you your (4) _____, which has your flight information. If you have a large bag or suitcase, you have to check it there. If you only have a (5) _____, you can take it on the plane with you. If you did (6) _____, you already have your boarding pass, so you can go straight to the (7) _____ in the departure area. You will have to go through a (8) _____ to make sure you don't have anything dangerous. Finally, when you get to your destination, you can pick up your checked bag from (9) _____.

### Grammar

| Expressing Prohibition | |
|---|---|
| Use *must not* to say something is not allowed. | You **must not** bring a knife on the plane. |
| *Must not* and *can't* both mean that something is not allowed. *Must not* is stronger, and is used for rules. | You **must not** open that door. You **can't** take a large piece of baggage as a carry-on. |

**C** Write sentences about traveling by plane. Use *have to, must, must not,* and *can't.*

1. _____

2. _____

3. _____

4. _____

5. _____

## Conversation

**Barajas International Airport in Madrid, Spain**

**D** 🎧 51 Listen to the conversation with your book closed. What time will the traveler get on the plane?

**Airline agent:** Good afternoon. Where are you flying to today?

**Traveler:** To Bogotá. Here's my passport.

**Airline agent:** Thank you. And do you have any bags to check?

**Traveler:** Just one. And this is my carry-on bag.

**Airline agent:** OK, thank you. Here's your boarding pass. You're in seat 27D. Boarding time is 10:15 at gate 13, but you must be at the gate 30 minutes before that.

**Traveler:** OK, and 27D is a window seat, isn't it?

**Airline agent:** No, I'm afraid it isn't. There aren't any window seats available.

**Traveler:** Oh, I thought I had reserved a window seat when I booked online.

**Airline agent:** I'm sorry about that, ma'am. Is there anything else I can help you with?

**Traveler:** Yes, is there a restaurant after the security check?

**Airline agent:** Yes, there are two. Thank you, and enjoy your flight!

**SPEAKING STRATEGY**

Notice the traveler's question: *27D is a window seat, isn't it?* Use these short questions at the end of a sentence to confirm information.

**E** In pairs, practice the conversation. Switch roles and practice it again.

---

✓ **GOAL CHECK** Use English at the Airport

1. In pairs, write a list of the things you do at an airport.

2. Join another pair and compare your lists. Put the actions in order.

3. Prepare the dialog for a how-to video in which you show other students how to use English at the airport.

# D  GOAL  Discuss Travel

## Reading

**A** **MY WORLD** What do you like about traveling? Is there anything you don't like about going somewhere you've never been before? Tell your partner.

**B** Scan the article, and add the phrases (a–d) to the paragraphs (1–4) to create subheadings.

**a.** is good for your health

**b.** promotes cultural understanding

**c.** takes you out of your comfort zone

**d.** helps you become a global citizen

**C** Read the article again. Circle **T** for *true* and **F** for *false*.

| | | |
|---|---|---|
| **1.** Your comfort zone is where you sleep. | **T** | **F** |
| **2.** Sightseeing can involve exercise. | **T** | **F** |
| **3.** Global citizens want to work together to solve the world's problems. | **T** | **F** |
| **4.** We can't learn about culture in restaurants, cafes, or markets. | **T** | **F** |
| **5.** We learn about ourselves when we travel. | **T** | **F** |

**D** Answer the questions.

**1.** Why are challenging situations sometimes good for us?

_____

**2.** Why is travel good for your mind and body?

_____

**3.** What does the term *global citizen* refer to?

_____

**4.** How do we learn about our own culture when we travel?

_____

**5.** Why is cultural understanding important?

_____

## ✓ GOAL CHECK

**1.** Remember a trip you have taken. Write notes to answer the questions.

> Where did you go, and how long did you stay?
>
> What was the most challenging / interesting / frightening / unusual moment of that trip?
>
> What did you learn during the trip?

**2.** Tell a partner about your trip.

# Four Reasons Why Traveling is Good for You

Taking a trip can be hard. There may be long lines at the airport, crowds at the security check, and uncomfortable seats at the gate, but traveling—meeting new people, visiting different places, and even eating different foods—is good for us in many ways. Here are four.

## 1. Travel _____

In our daily lives, we generally know where we're going to go, what we're going to do, and who we're going to see. We know where to go and who to ask if we need something, and we know *how* to ask for that something. We're in our comfort zone; we're comfortable. When we travel to a different country, where people might speak a different language, we leave our comfort zone, and sometimes that can be frightening. Things are different, and some things will be challenging. But it's worth it! Challenges help us grow and become more confident.

## 2. Travel _____

Changes in location and breaks from our routine make us feel better. We are **stimulated** by seeing new places, trying new food, and experiencing new cultures. Also, when we travel, we are often more active, so we do more exercise, even if it is only walking around a new city sightseeing. Traveling can be very **motivating** and exciting, so it is good for your mind and your body.

## 3. Travel _____

There are a lot of problems in our world that will cause bigger problems in the future if we don't find solutions. With climate change, pollution, and other environmental issues in front of us, we need to work together as **citizens** *of the world*, not just citizens of our own country. When you travel, you meet new people, make new connections, and understand the world better. This helps you become a global citizen.

## 4. Travel _____

When we travel, we can visit museums, art galleries, and festivals, as well as restaurants, cafes, and markets. All these things help us learn about the history and culture of a country and help us understand that people around the world think differently and do things differently. When we travel, we learn about a country, its culture, and its people, and we come home with new understanding. This opportunity to experience other cultures opens your mind and can help you respect others and see your own culture more clearly.

So, whether you go on vacation, take a business trip, or study abroad, travel is good for you. Where will *you* go next?

**stimulate** to make someone excited and interested about something
**motivating** makes you want to do something
**citizen** a person who lives in a particular place

**Pedestrian-friendly street in Oaxaca, Mexico**

# E   GOAL   Describe a Cultural Event

## Communication

**A**  Read the text. What cultural festivals or events do you know about? Write a list.

### Hawaii's Lantern Floating Festival

People travel from all over the world to participate in Hawaii's Lantern Floating festival. Lantern Floating is a ceremony to remember family and friends who have died. It takes place on Memorial Day, the last Monday in May. The festival begins with music and singing, and then, as the sun sets, everyone lights their lanterns. Each lantern has a message written on it, and sometimes people also attach photos of their loved ones to them. Once they are lit, the lanterns are released onto the water. It is a truly beautiful sight. Lantern Floating is a moment to remember and give thanks to the people who have left the world before us.

**B**  Choose an event from your list, and write notes about it. Use the questions.

When does it take place?

Where does it take place?

What is it for?

What do people do?

Do people come from far away to go to the event?

How would you describe it? Write three adjectives.

> What's the name of your event?

> Day of the Dead.

> When does Day of the Dead take place?

**The annual Lantern Floating ceremony is held at Ala Moana Beach Park in Oahu, Hawaii.**

Ask a partner about their cultural event.

## Writing

 Read the text about a festival. <u>Underline</u> the topic sentence and the last sentence.

### Nevada's Burning Man Art Festival

Every August, thousands of people from America and around the world travel to Black Rock Desert, Nevada, in the US. They travel there to participate in Burning Man, a huge festival that celebrates community, creativity, and art. There aren't any hotels or stores nearby, so people camp and have to bring everything they need with them. A temporary community is created for a week in the middle of the desert—it's incredible! Some people come to look at and experience the art, but others come to create it. They construct enormous pieces of unusual art in the middle of the desert. It's an amazing sight. At the end of the week, many of the creations are burned. This tradition comes from the very first Burning Man in 1986, where an 8-foot-tall (2.4 m) wooden man was burned. A giant figure of a man is still burned on the last night of the event each year. So, if you like travel, art, and unusual experiences, you should visit Burning Man next August! You can't make a hotel reservation, but you have to book a ticket online for the festival.

WRITING STRATEGY

The topic sentence (the introduction) and the last sentence (the conclusion) work together. They both need to show the main idea of the paragraph.

 Use your notes from **B** to write a text for a travel blog. In your blog, you want to encourage people to visit your country for the cultural event. Use the text in **D** to help you.

 Exchange texts with a partner. How can your partner improve his or her text? Write notes on the text. Use your partner's comments to make corrections and improvements.

## ✓ GOAL CHECK Describe a Cultural Event

1. In small groups, share your texts.

2. Discuss the different cultural events and decide which one you would all like to visit. Explain your reasons to the class.

I would like to visit... because...

# VIDEO JOURNAL

# TEDTALKS

## WHY ART THRIVES AT BURNING MAN

**NORA ATKINSON**
Craft Curator

Nora Atkinson's **idea worth spreading** is that the value of art should not come from its price but from its ability to inspire curiosity, engagement, and collaboration. Watch Atkinson's TED Talk on TED.com.

**A** Discuss the question in pairs. What kind of art do you like?

> drawing        graffiti        painting
> photography    sculpture

**B** Match the words and expressions to their meanings. Write the letter.

1. thrive ☐                       a. people will want to buy it

2. throw your back into something ☐       b. it won't match or look good in your home

3. marketable ☐                   c. be very successful

4. it doesn't go with the sofa ☐   d. try really hard to do something

**C** Watch the first part of the video. Circle T for true and F for false.

1. Atkinson is describing a large piece of art that was created in the desert.        T    F

2. A group of people pulled ropes to stop the wheel from moving.        T    F

3. Peter Hudson is an artist.        T    F

4. Nora thinks people will want to buy this work of art.        T    F

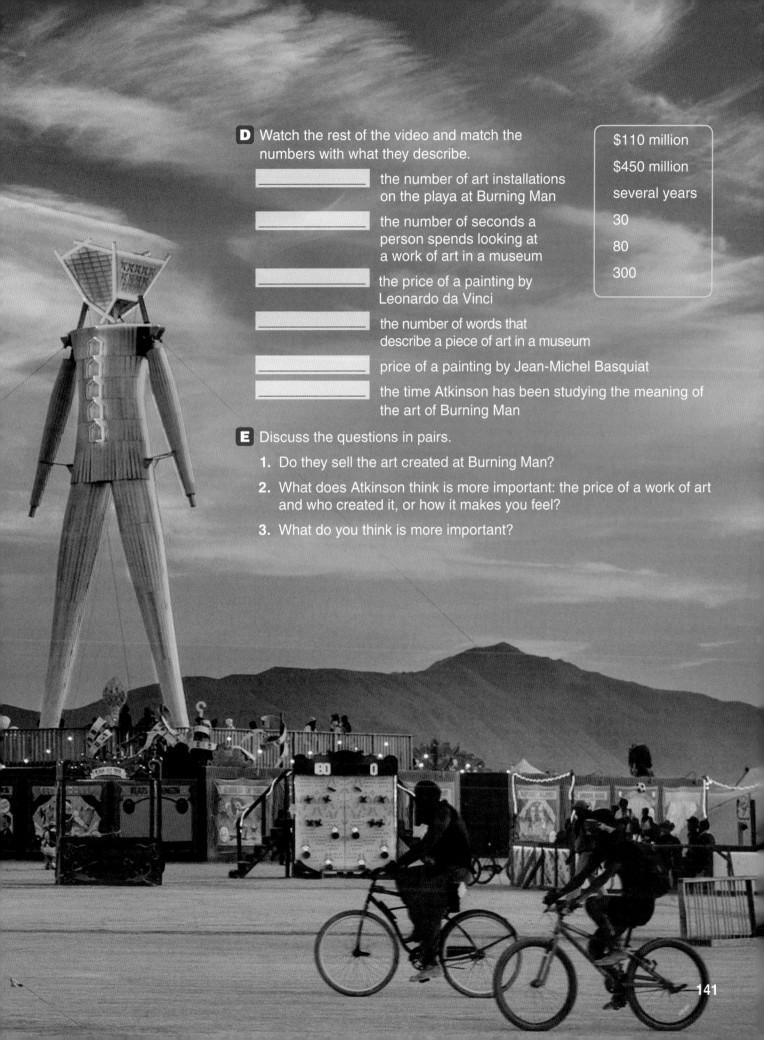

**D** Watch the rest of the video and match the numbers with what they describe.

$110 million

$450 million

several years

30

80

300

_____ the number of art installations on the playa at Burning Man

_____ the number of seconds a person spends looking at a work of art in a museum

_____ the price of a painting by Leonardo da Vinci

_____ the number of words that describe a piece of art in a museum

_____ price of a painting by Jean-Michel Basquiat

_____ the time Atkinson has been studying the meaning of the art of Burning Man

**E** Discuss the questions in pairs.

1. Do they sell the art created at Burning Man?

2. What does Atkinson think is more important: the price of a work of art and who created it, or how it makes you feel?

3. What do you think is more important?

# Careers

Mira Nakashima, a designer
and woodworker, in New Hope,
Pennsylvania

**Look at the photo and answer the questions:**

**1** What is the person in the photo doing? Why?

**2** What knowledge and skills does this person have?

## UNIT 11 GOALS

**A.** Discuss Career Choices

**B.** Ask and Answer Job-Related Questions

**C.** Talk about Career Planning

**D.** Explain New Careers

**E.** Create a Personal Profile

143

# **GOAL** Discuss Career Choices

## Vocabulary

**A** 🎧 53 Listen to a conversation between a high school senior and a career advisor. What does Marcy do at the hospital?

**B** 🎧 53 Listen again. Then, fill in the blanks in Ms. Carter's notes below with the words in the box.

| | | | |
|---|---|---|---|
| assistant | boss | employee | experience |
| owner | qualifications | training | volunteer |

This modern, open-concept office space encourages collaboration, creativity, and innovation.

- Marcy has some work (1) _____. She went through a (2) _____ program to become a family (3) _____ at the hospital. It's (4) _____ work, so Marcy doesn't get paid.

- Marcy would like to be a business (5) _____, but she doesn't have the necessary (6) _____ yet.

- I explained that she could start as an (7) _____ at a business. Later, perhaps, she can be the (8) _____ when she has her own business.

**C** Complete each sentence with a word from **B**.

1. An _____ works for an employer.
2. If you do _____ work, you don't get paid.
3. In a _____ program, you learn how to do something.
4. If you are the _____ of a company, it is your company.
5. An _____ helps you.

**D** In pairs, discuss what you think Marcy should do to prepare for her future. What degrees or training should she get?

> I think she should study more.

> Yes, she should get a degree in business administration.

**E** **MY WORLD** In pairs, talk about the education or experience that you have. Use the information in the box to help you.

| | |
|---|---|
| bachelor's degree | extracurricular activities |
| vocational degree | volunteer work |

## Grammar

| Modals for Giving Advice | |
|---|---|
| We use *should* + verb to say that something is (or isn't) a good idea. | You **should choose** a career that fits your personality. You **shouldn't apply** for an office job if you don't like to be inside all day. |
| Use *had better* to say that something bad could happen if the advice isn't followed. | You **had better** prepare well for your interview. He**'d better** practice his English before he goes. |
| Use *maybe, perhaps,* or *I think* with modals to make the advice sound gentler and friendlier. | **Maybe** you **should become** a health-care worker. |

**F** Complete the sentences with an advice modal. Use a negative form when necessary.

1. You _____ listen to your boss!

2. Juan _____ finish the course so he can get his degree.

3. The employees _____ leave early when the boss isn't there.

4. Perhaps you _____ look for a job as an assistant first.

5. Martha _____ do the training program if she's not interested in the job.

**G** Complete the sentences in pairs. Use your own ideas.

> ### Career Advice
>
> - If you want to become a successful business owner, you should _____, but you _____ shouldn't _____.
> - If you want to get a degree, you had better _____.
> - You should _____ if you want to get some work experience. Good luck!

**H** Read one of the problems out loud to a partner. Your partner will give you friendly advice using *maybe, perhaps,* or *I think.*

1. I don't know what career to choose.
2. I don't have any experience.
3. I want to get a better job.

4. My job doesn't pay very well.
5. My job application was rejected.
6. I need an assistant to help me at work.

 **GOAL CHECK** Discuss Career Choices

1. Look at the careers in the box. What training, experience, and other qualifications are needed for each career? Choose three and write notes.

2. In pairs, discuss each career.

3. Would you choose any of these careers? Why?

> App developer
> Computer systems analyst
> Health services manager
> Market research analyst
> Physical therapist
> Sales representative

# GOAL Ask and Answer Job-Related Questions

## Listening

**A** 🎧 54 Listen to an interview with a restaurant owner. Why did he start his own business?

**B** 🎧 54 Listen again and answer the questions.

1. When did Mr. Sangumram open the New Thailand restaurant? _____

2. Who is the cook at the restaurant? _____

3. What kind of food is served at the restaurant? _____

4. How far from the owner's home is the restaurant? _____

5. How many employees work at the restaurant? _____

6. What does Mr. Sangumram's wife do for a living? _____

**C** What makes a good job? Rank the following from 1 (most important) to 6 (least important). Share your answers in pairs.

_____ amount of vacation time          _____ distance from home

_____ wage or salary level             _____ long-term employment

_____ working alone or with others     _____ interesting job duties

**Thai restaurant cook working in a restaurant**

**D** **MY WORLD** Do you have a job at the moment? Have you had a job in the past? Tell a partner about your job(s).

## PRONUNCIATION: Intonation in Questions

In *yes/no* questions, the speaker's voice rises on the last content word.

**Does your wife work with you at the restaurant?**

In questions with *wh-* words, the speaker's voice rises on the first content word and falls on the last content word.

**When did you open this wonderful restaurant?**

**E** 🎧 55 Listen and repeat the questions. Then, ask and answer them in pairs.

1. What do Mr. Sangumram's children do? _____

2. Does his wife work at the restaurant? _____

3. What does his nephew do? _____

4. Does the restaurant serve Chinese food? _____

5. Where do Mr. and Mrs. Sangumram live? _____

6. Does Mr. Sangumram enjoy his job? _____

## Communication

**F** When you are looking for a job, what do you want to know? Write a question for each one.

| What I want to know about: | Questions I can ask: |
|---|---|
| Salary | |
| Training opportunities | |
| Vacation time | |
| Travel opportunities | |
| Hours | |

**Diving Instructor:**

Understands and teaches the use of scuba equipment.

Works outdoors.

Should be a strong swimmer.

Salary varies by season.

**Commercial Pilot:**

Knows about airplane mechanics, weather, radio communication.

Works long hours.

Often far away from home.

**Market Research Analyst:**

Should be interested in psychology and behavior.

Works under pressure.

Should have strong organizational and communication skills.

**G** Read the job profiles in the box. Choose one that you are interested in. Tell a partner why you chose that job.

## GOAL CHECK
## Ask and Answer Job-Related Questions

Join another pair and ask and answer each other's questions in **F** about the different jobs.

> What qualifications should a market research analyst have?

> Well, a degree in communications or business administration is useful.

## C  GOAL  Talk about Career Planning

### Language Expansion: Participial Adjectives

**A** Read the article. What are the noun forms of the words in blue?

**Flight medics prepare for takeoff.**

A. J. Coston isn't waiting to start his dream job. At age 18, he's a weekend volunteer firefighter in the United States. During the week, he lives at home with his mom, dad, and sister, and does his main job: going to high school. "I have always wanted to get into firefighting... since I was a little kid watching fire trucks go by," he says. "One day I was bored and on the internet, and I found out that Loudoun County offered a junior firefighter program."

Some of A. J.'s friends are surprised by his decision to spend weekends at the firehouse, but to A. J., helping people is more satisfying than anything else. The job is never boring, either, since firefighters get called to all sorts of emergencies. One terrifying moment for A. J. was getting an emergency call after four children were struck by lightning. Luckily, all four survived.

A. J. will be off to college next fall, and plans to study what he's most interested in: emergency medical care. "I want to be a flight medic on a helicopter eventually," he says.

**B** For each participial adjective in blue above, decide whether it describes (1) someone's feelings or (2) something that causes a certain feeling.

**1.** Describes someone's feelings: _____

**2.** Describes what causes the feeling: _____

### Grammar

| Indefinite Pronouns | |
|---|---|
| Pronouns refer to specified nouns. | **My boss** should hire an assistant. <br> **She** has too much work. |
| Indefinite pronouns refer to unspecified nouns. | **Somebody / Someone** has applied for the job. (I don't know who applied.) |
| Indefinite pronouns always take the singular form of a verb. Use *anybody / anyone* for questions and negative statements. Use *nobody / no one* to refer to not a single person from a group. Use *everybody / everyone* to refer to all of a group of people. | Has **anybody / anyone** met the new assistant? He doesn't know **anybody / anyone** at his new workplace. <br> **Nobody / No one** has met him yet. <br> **Everybody / Everyone** wants to meet him. |
| For places and things, use *somewhere / something, anywhere / anything, nowhere / nothing, everywhere / everything.* | If you want to get a job, you should do **something** to get some volunteer experience. Work experience is required **everywhere**. |

**C** Circle the correct indefinite pronoun.

1. Does *anybody* / *anything* want to do this training program?

2. *Somebody* / *Something* said the course was boring, but I think it looks interesting.

3. *Anyone* / *Everyone* is satisfied with the salary increase. *No one* / *Everyone* complained; they are all happy about it.

4. Is *anyone* / *anywhere* going to the meeting?

5. Is *something* / *everything* ready for the presentation? It starts in 5 minutes!

**D** <u>Underline</u> the indefinite pronoun and write the correct form of the verb in parentheses.

1. It's difficult to choose someone for the job because everyone _____ strong skills and experience. (have)

2. When you are applying for a job, everything _____ important. (be)

3. Somebody _____ information about the training program. Can you tell them about it? (want)

4. Nobody _____ the new online system; everybody _____ it is very confusing. (like, think)

## Conversation

**E** 🎧 56 **Listen to the conversation. What is the man planning to do?**

**Sam:** What do you want to do when you finish school?

**Isabel:** I'm not sure. What are you planning to do?

**Sam:** I want to do a training program somebody told me about. I'll learn about web design and app development, then I'll be able to get a job in that area.

**Isabel:** That sounds cool. You should definitely do it.

**Sam:** I know, but what about you? Have you asked anybody for advice about career planning?

**Isabel:** No... I should talk to someone, right?

**Sam:** Maybe you should talk to the career advisor at school.

**Isabel:** OK, I'll start planning, I promise!

**SPEAKING STRATEGY**

Notice Sam's question: *What about you?* We use this question to turn the conversation to the other person.

## ✓ GOAL CHECK Talk about Career Planning

1. What kind of career would be interesting and satisfying to you? Why? Write down some ideas and your reasons.

2. Answer the questions about your career choice. Write notes. Then, talk in pairs about your career planning.

   • How can you plan for this career?

   • What should you do in preparation?

   • Has anybody given you any advice?

   • Is there anything you can do to get experience?

# D GOAL Explain New Careers

## Reading

**A** Which industries do you think are going to grow most in the next ten years? Discuss in pairs.

> education      engineering      manufacturing
> medicine      technology

**B** Scan the article and choose the best option for the main idea.

**a.** Job duties are changing.

**b.** Adaptability, innovation, and creativity are important for getting a job.

**c.** New careers are developing.

**d.** Innovation and creativity are important in technology.

**C** Read the article. Complete the ideas.

**1.** We need to learn new skills because
_____.

**2.** Innovative means that _____
_____.

**3.** Social and environmental issues are
_____.

**4.** Travel vloggers _____
_____.

**5.** Digital skills _____.

## ✓ GOAL CHECK

**1.** Choose a career from the box and answer the questions. Write notes.

> data scientist      media specialist
> social media manager      user experience designer

- What do you think this career involves?

- What specific skills would you need?

- Why do you need to be adaptable, innovative, and creative for this career?

**2.** Talk about the different careers in groups.

# Changing Careers

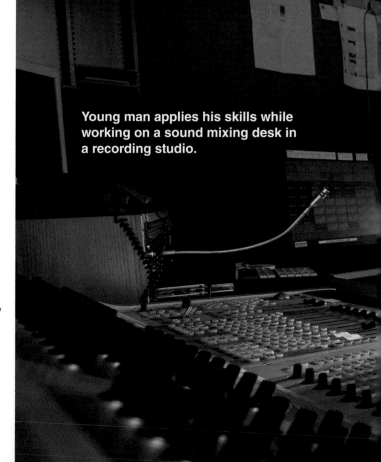

As technology grows, job profiles change. Consequently, the skills you need are changing and new careers are opening up. In the past, people used to prepare for a career that would lead to a job for life, but now we need to be able to **adapt** to change.

So, how can we plan our careers? What new career choices can we make? First of all, it is important to be adaptable. Job duties are changing, so we need to be able to learn new skills. We also need to be innovative and creative. This means we need to have new, interesting ideas and think of different ways to do things because that's what employers are looking for. They want employees who can **think outside the box** and help their companies face the new challenges of the digital age.

**Young man applies his skills while working on a sound mixing desk in a recording studio.**

However, it is not only employers who are looking for different skills; future employees are also looking for different things. Many young people are worried about social and environmental issues, and they want a career that will help them make the world a better place. So, they are looking for companies that also care about change and social responsibility. They are also looking for flexibility and opportunities to be creative. They don't want a boring job where they will be sitting at a desk in an office all day, every day. They want challenging careers where they'll be doing different things in different places.

So what kind of innovative, exciting careers are there for these new generations? App developer, social media manager, travel vlogger, user experience designer, data scientist, and video and media specialist are some of them.

Let's take a look at a couple of these careers. What does it take to be an app developer? Obviously, you need to be innovative and creative, and understand programming and mobile platforms, but what might make you **stand out**?

For example, you could connect your interest in technology to your interest in environmental issues and design an app to help people create a **car pool** system at their workplace.

For a travel vlogger, traveling the world is part of the job, but you need to be creative too, because the other part of the job is to take photos, make videos, and write interesting texts about your travels. Companies in the travel and tourism industry will pay to use your vlog as part of their **marketing**. However, this career is also an opportunity to work for the issues you're interested in. Photographers who travel the world taking photos of nature can use vlogging to help people understand conservation issues.

We've just looked at two new areas here, but from them we can see that job profiles are changing, and new careers are developing. So, if you're planning your career, or thinking about changing careers, remember the importance of being adaptable, innovative, and creative, and the possibilities for taking advantage of your digital skills.

**adapt** change your way of doing things for a new situation
**think outside the box** think imaginatively, to find unexpected or creative solutions
**stand out** be noticed as better than others
**car pool** a group of people take turns driving so they only use one car to travel to work
**marketing** what a company does to try to convince people to buy its products or services

# GOAL Create a Personal Profile

## Communication

**A** Why do people decide to change careers? Write a list of possible reasons.

**B** You have decided you want to change careers. Write notes about your decision. Use the questions to help you.

- What is your current job?
- Why do you want to change careers?
- What ideas do you have for a new career?
- What should you do to prepare for this career change?

**C** Give a partner advice about changing careers. Use *should* and *had better*.

**Soyoung Lee is the curator of the Metropolitan Museum's department of Asian Art in New York.**

> Why do you want to change careers?

> I'm bored of doing the same thing every day. My job isn't satisfying. I need a change.

> Maybe you should look for something that is more exciting. Do you know anyone in the tourism industry? You had better ...

# Writing

**D** Circle the correct words to complete the text.

Sometimes people decide to change careers because they don't feel (1) *challenging / challenged*. Often, they have been doing the same job for many years and it has become (2) *boring / bored*. And let's be honest, (3) *nobody / anybody* wants to continue in a job that isn't (4) *satisfying / satisfied*. That's when you should look for (5) *something / someone* new and more (6) *exciting / excited*. (7) *Everybody / Anybody* has skills and knowledge that will help them start a new job or career. Before you start applying for different jobs, one of the things you (8) *should / shouldn't* do is write your personal profile for your resume. This is a short paragraph—it (9) *should / shouldn't* be more than 100 words—that says who you are, what experience and skills you have, and your career goals.

**E** Complete the personal profile with the words in the box.

> challenging    digital    innovative    interested    manager    marketing

I am a (1) _____ graduate specializing in social media marketing. I have significant experience with tour companies and hotels, and have developed my design and (2) _____ skills through these marketing projects. I'm (3) _____ in finding a (4) _____ position as a social media (5) _____ where I can use my creativity to develop (6) _____ ways of using social media for the company's growth.

**WRITING STRATEGY**

A personal profile should include three things:
1. Who you are (*I am a marketing graduate specializing in...*)
2. What you can offer the company (*I have significant experience with...*)
3. Your professional goals (*I'm interested in finding a challenging position...*)

**F** Answer these questions in your notebook.

1. Are you a recent graduate / technician / office worker / engineer / _____ ?
2. What qualifications, training, and experience do you have?
3. What other skills do you have?
4. What kind of position (job) are you looking for?

**G** Use your notes in **F** to write your personal profile. Use the model in **E** to help you.

---

 **GOAL CHECK** Create a Personal Profile

1. In small groups, share your profiles.
2. Are the profiles interesting?

> I am a social media influencer with over 9,000 followers.

> Wow! I had no idea!

# VIDEO JOURNAL

## JOEL SARTORE: THE PHOTO ARK

**A** In pairs, discuss what you think are the advantages or disadvantages of being a photographer. Do you think a photographer's work is easy or difficult? Why? What makes you remember a photo?

**B** Match the words to their meanings. Write the letter.

1. portrait ____    a. something behind something else
2. extinct ____    b. no longer in existence
3. conservation ____    c. a group of 12
4. dozen ____    d. a painting or photograph of someone posing
5. species ____    e. a group of living things; a type, a category
6. background ____    f. protection, especially of nature

**C** Watch the video. Answer the questions.

1. Write five animals you see.
   _____
2. Does Joel only take pictures of animals?
   _____
3. Which pictures are the most important to him?
   _____
   _____

**D** Watch the video again. Complete the information.

1. Joel has worked with National Geographic for over _____.
2. Joel started taking pictures in _____.

3. Now Joel is working on a _____ called The Photo Ark.
4. Joel's portraits give animals of different sizes an _____ voice; there is no _____ comparison.
5. Joel's conservation heroes are people with _____ and _____.
6. Joel doesn't think about the world in _____ years; he thinks about it _____.

**E** Discuss the questions in pairs.

1. How do you feel looking at the portraits of animals that are now extinct?
2. Why does Joel think about the world today instead of in fifty years?

**F** Research a National Geographic explorer in pairs.

- Name
- Nationality
- Area of interest
- Where have they explored?
- Years with the National Geographic Society
- What does it take to be a National Geographic explorer?

**G** Present your explorer to the class.

# Celebrations

Chinese dancers wear traditional costumes for Spring Festival celebrations at a temple fair in Beijing, China.

## UNIT 12 GOALS

**A.** Describe a Celebration

**B.** Compare Holidays in Different Countries

**C.** Express Congratulations and Good Wishes

**D.** Talk about Rituals

**E.** Share Opinions about Holidays

## A GOAL Describe a Celebration

### Vocabulary

**A** Read about a special New Year's celebration.

New Year's Day is a holiday around the world, but people in Edinburgh, Scotland, celebrate it in an exciting way. They have a festival called Hogmanay. Hogmanay takes place all around the city, from December 29th to January 1st. It starts with a parade on the night of December 29th. On December 30th, there are concerts and dancing. Finally, on New Year's Eve, there is a street party with fireworks, and people wear very colorful costumes. There is always a big crowd, even though it's very cold. One year, more than 100,000 people participated. The celebration in Edinburgh is very well-known, but the annual Hogmanay festivals in other cities in Scotland are popular, too.

Fireworks on Calton Hill during Edinburgh's Hogmanay in Edinburgh, Scotland

**B** Write the words in blue next to the correct meaning.

1. _____ : happens

2. _____ : famous

3. _____ : a day when people don't work

4. _____ : a large group of people

5. _____ : happening once each year

6. _____ : special clothes for a performance

7. _____ : do something enjoyable for a special day

8. _____ : took part in

**C** Would you like to participate in Hogmanay in Edinburgh? Why? Discuss in pairs.

> I would like to participate in Hogmanay because I love music and dancing. How about you?

> No, I wouldn't like it. I don't like big crowds.

**D** Complete the paragraph with words from **A**.

China also (1) _____ New Year in an exciting way, but it is at a different time of year than Hogmanay. It always (2) _____ in January or February. New Year is the most important Chinese (3) _____, and most people don't have to work. The (4) _____ celebrations include a big meal with family, a gift of money in a red envelope for children, and fireworks. One of the most (5) _____ traditions of Chinese New Year is the dragon or lion dance. There is always a big (6) _____ watching the dance.

**E** **MY WORLD** How do you celebrate New Year's Day? Discuss in pairs.

## Grammar

### Comparisons with *as ... as*

| Subject + *be* + | *(not) as* + adjective + *as* + | complement |
|---|---|---|
| New Year's Day is | **as** exciting **as** | Independence Day. (The two holidays are equally exciting.) |
| Hogmanay is | **not as** popular **as** | Carnival. (Hogmanay is less popular than Carnival; Carnival is more popular than Hogmanay.) |
| Use *as ... as* to say that two things are equal. Use *not as ... as* to say that two things are not equal. | | |

**F** Write sentences with *(not) as ... as* to compare the two festivals.

| | **The Spring Festival** | **The Harvest Fair** |
|---|---|---|
| **1.** old | started in 1970 | started in 1970 |
| **2.** long | 2 days | 4 days |
| **3.** popular | 5,000 people | 5,000 people |
| **4.** expensive | tickets are $15 | tickets are $30 |
| **5.** big | 10 concerts | 23 concerts |
| **6.** well-known | on a few local TV shows | on the internet |

> **WORD FOCUS**
>
> A **festival** is a type of celebration; for example, the Festival of Colors is celebrated in India in March.
>
> A **festival** can also be an event that you pay to go to.

**1.** The Spring Festival _is as old as the Harvest Fair_____.

**2.** The Spring Festival _____.

**3.** _____.

**4.** _____.

**5.** _____.

**6.** _____.

**G** Choose two celebrations that you know. Compare them using *as ... as.*

## ✔ GOAL CHECK  Describe a Celebration

**1.** What is your favorite celebration?

**2.** Why is it your favorite celebration and how do you celebrate it? Complete the graphic organizer.

**3.** Tell a partner about your favorite celebration.

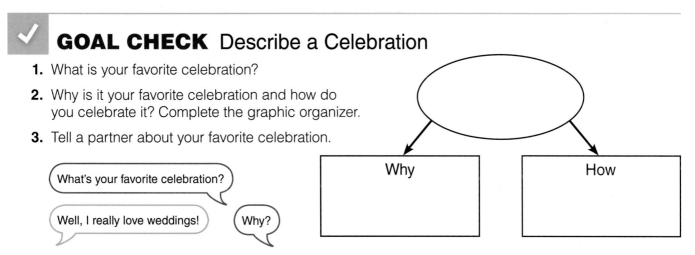

What's your favorite celebration?

Well, I really love weddings!     Why?

Why     How

# B GOAL Compare Holidays in Different Countries

## Listening

**A** 🎧 58 Listen to three people talk about a holiday in their country. Number the countries in the order that you hear about them.

**a.** Japan _____     **b.** Mexico _____     **c.** United States _____

**B** 🎧 58 Listen again and fill in the charts.

---

**The Day of the Dead**

Country:
_____

When is it?
_____

How do people celebrate it?
**a.** go to the cemetery with
_____

**b.** bring
_____

What is the special food?
**a.** sweet
_____

**b.** candy
_____

---

**Halloween**

Country:
_____

When is it?
_____

How do people celebrate it?
**a.** put on
_____

**b.** ask for
_____

**c.** watch
_____

What is the special food?
**a.** _____

**b.** _____

---

**O-Bon**

Country:
_____

When is it?
_____

How do people celebrate it?
**a.** go back to
_____

**b.** participate in a special
_____

**c.** make big
_____

---

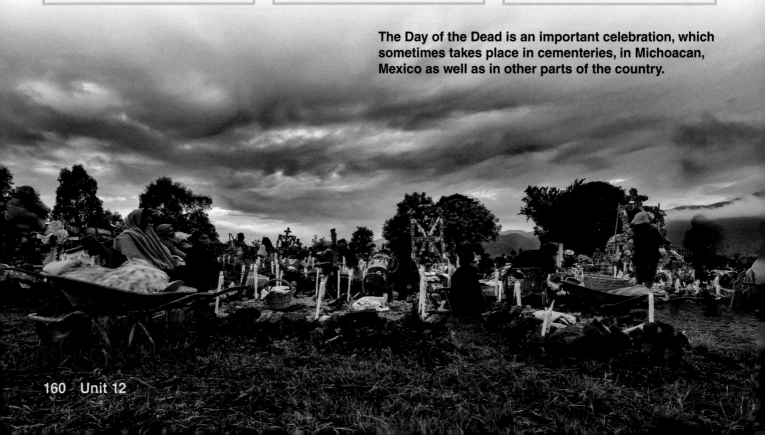

The Day of the Dead is an important celebration, which sometimes takes place in cementeries, in Michoacan, Mexico as well as in other parts of the country.

**C** **MY WORLD** Is there a special holiday in your country to remember people who have died? Discuss in pairs.

**D** Discuss these questions in pairs.

1. Do you know about any other holidays like these in other countries?

2. Why do you think different countries have similar holidays?

## Pronunciation: Question Intonation with Lists

**E** 🎧 59 Listen to the questions. Notice how the intonation rises and falls in questions with a list of choices.

1. Would you like to go on holiday in Mexico, the US, or Japan?

2. Is O-Bon in July or August?

**F** 🎧 60 Read the questions and mark the intonation with arrows. Then, listen and check your answers. Finally, ask and answer the questions in pairs.

1. Is the Day of the Dead on November 1st or 2nd?

2. On the Day of the Dead, do people eat sweet bread, chocolate, or fruit?

3. Is Halloween for children or adults?

4. What do you like the most: the costumes, the candies, or the scary movies?

5. Is O-Bon in August or September?

6. At O-Bon, are there fireworks, bonfires, or both?

## Communication

**G** In groups, imagine that you can take a trip to participate in one of the holidays in **A**. Discuss these questions.

1. How are these holidays similar? Think of as many answers as you can.

2. How are they different?

3. What could visitors do at each holiday?

4. Which holiday would you like to participate in? Why?

 **GOAL CHECK**
## Compare Holidays in Different Countries

1. Which holiday did you choose in **G**? With your group, make a list of reasons why you chose that holiday.

2. Now make a list of reasons why you didn't choose the other two holidays.

3. Explain your decision to the class. Say why you chose the holiday, and why you didn't choose the others.

> We don't want to go to the Day of the Dead in Mexico because ...

> So, we chose to go to O-Bon in Japan. We think ...

> We want to go to O-Bon because ...

# GOAL Express Congratulations and Good Wishes

## Language Expansion: Expressions for Celebrations

**A** Read the expressions and how we use them.

| Expression | Use it |
|---|---|
| Congratulations! | when someone is getting married, having a baby, getting a promotion, wins a game, etc. |
| Well done! Great job! | when someone has accomplished something difficult (passed a driving test, an exam, etc.). |
| Good luck! | to wish someone a good result or a good future. |
| Happy Birthday / Anniversary / New Year! | to greet someone or wish them the best on a holiday or special occasion. |

**B** Write the correct expression for each situation in your notebook.

1. Your friend has to take a difficult exam tomorrow.

2. You're leaving someone's house after a Thanksgiving meal.

3. Your neighbor tells you he plans to get married soon.

4. Today is your friend's birthday. You see your friend.

5. Your friend got an excellent grade on an exam.

6. It is midnight on December 31st in London.

**Hands with henna design for a wedding ceremony in Abu Dhabi, Dubai**

## Grammar

| Would rather | |
|---|---|
| Use *would rather* + base form of the verb to talk about actions we prefer. | I **would rather have** a small wedding than a big wedding. |
| Use *would rather not* + base form of the verb to talk about things we don't want to do. | I**'d rather not have** a party for my birthday. |
| Use *would rather* + base form of the verb in *yes* / *no* questions to ask people about their preferences. | **Would you rather see** Chinese New Year or Hogmanay? |

C Use *I'd rather* to write sentences about things you would like to do on your birthday.

1. have (a big party / a small party) *I'd rather have a big party than a small party.*

2. eat (at home / in a restaurant) _____

3. invite (lots of people / a few close friends) _____

4. get (flowers / presents) _____

5. wear (nice clothes / jeans and a T-shirt) _____

D Ask a partner about his or her preferences. Use the choices in **C** and *Would you rather ...?*

## Conversation

E 🎧 61 Listen to the conversation. What are they going to celebrate?

**Mike:** Hi Katie! Congratulations on your new job!

**Katie:** Thanks, Mike. It was a really challenging interview, but I guess I did OK!

**Mike:** Well done! We should celebrate. Would you rather go out or invite a few friends to your house?

**Katie:** I think I'd rather go out for dinner. We can invite Lucia and Ana.

**Mike:** OK. I'll book a table at Italiano's.

**Katie:** Italiano's? I'd rather go somewhere quieter.

**SPEAKING STRATEGY**

Notice Katie's answer to Mike's question about what she'd like to do: *I think I'd rather go out for dinner.* We often use *I think* at the beginning to make an answer less direct and more polite.

F Practice the conversation in pairs. Then, make new conversations. Change the situation and how you are going to celebrate.

## GOAL CHECK
## Express Congratulations and Good Wishes

1. Think of three situations in which you would congratulate or give someone good wishes.

2. In pairs, decide which expressions from **A** you would use.

3. Prepare the script for an etiquette guide video to show other students how to express congratulations and good wishes in English in different situations.

# **GOAL** Talk about Rituals

## Reading

**A** Look at the title and the photo. What is a ritual? What do you think the woman in the photo is celebrating? Discuss in pairs.

**B** Scan the article and write the phrases in the correct paragraph.

    **a.** Turning to baby showers, in Ancient Greece and Egypt,

    **b.** Bridal showers celebrate the bride,

    **c.** Nowadays, both celebrations

    **d.** This tradition of giving gifts to the bride

**C** Read the article. Circle **T** for *true* or **F** for *false*.

    **1.** Bridal and baby showers are modern rituals.     **T**    **F**

    **2.** The bride's family usually organizes the shower.     **T**    **F**

    **3.** The tradition of playing games at a baby shower began in the 19th century.     **T**    **F**

    **4.** People have always given gifts before the baby is born.     **T**    **F**

    **5.** Baby showers help people get the things they need for their new baby.     **T**    **F**

    **6.** The future father is always invited to the shower these days.     **T**    **F**

 **GOAL CHECK**

Discuss the questions in groups.

    **1.** What do baby and wedding showers have in common?

    **2.** What do you think about men being involved in wedding and baby showers (as the future husbands or fathers, or as guests)?

    **3.** How do you think baby and wedding showers might change over the next twenty years?

    **4.** What special rituals for weddings and births are there in your country?

# The Rituals of Life Events

Weddings and births have always been important moments for families and society. Not surprisingly, they involve celebrations and rituals. Apart from the religious rituals in many cultures for both of these events, typical celebrations also include the bridal shower and the baby shower. Many people think of these showers as modern rituals, but in fact both of them have their **roots** in history.

_____ the woman who is getting married, and they are usually organized by a close friend. The people invited are female friends and members of her family. There will be food and drinks, and the women will share stories, express their good wishes, and sometimes give advice. But perhaps the most important ritual is the "showering of gifts," when the guests all give presents to the bride-to-be.

_____ is believed to have begun in Holland in the 16th century. The story is that the daughter of a rich man fell in love with a poor man, but her father didn't want her to marry him. He **refused** to give her a **dowry** if she married the poor man. So her friends and family and people from the village all gave her gifts so that she could get married. Since then, it has been a custom for the bride to receive presents from her family and friends before her wedding. However, the word _shower_ wasn't used until the 18th century, when it became popular to put the gifts in an open paper **parasol** and "shower" them over the bride.

_____ mothers were always **accompanied** by a group of women during and after the birth. One of their rituals was to offer gifts to the goddess of birth after the baby was born, as well as give useful gifts and food to the new mother. Pregnant women continued to be celebrated over the years, and in the 19th century the celebration developed into a tea party with gifts and games, after the birth of the baby. Finally, in the 20th century, after the Second World War, baby showers became more like they are today. Friends and family organize a shower before the baby is born, and people give the mother-to-be practical gifts to help her and the baby. The gift giving and the fun games are two customs that remain part of the baby shower ritual.

_____ often involve men, too. At a wedding shower, close friends and family sometimes celebrate the couple together before their marriage. And at a baby shower, both future parents might be there. There may also be male guests. Although the way we celebrate these important moments has changed over time, baby showers and bridal or wedding showers are part of the rituals surrounding these two important life events.

**roots** where something comes from, its origins
**refuse** say no to something
**dowry** an amount of money that a woman's parents give to the man she marries
**parasol** a kind of umbrella to protect you from the sun
**accompany** go or be with someone

# GOAL  Share Opinions about Holidays

## Communication

**A** What holidays do you celebrate? What do you and your family do for these celebrations? Discuss in pairs.

I agree.
I'm not sure.
I disagree.

**B** Write your opinion about these sentences in your notebook. Use the expressions in the box.

1. A new holiday isn't a real holiday.

2. Some old holidays are not very important now.

3. Our country should start a new holiday.

4. People spend too much money on holidays.

5. It's very important to keep all of the old holiday customs.

## Writing

**C** Read about how to write an opinion paragraph.

| WRITING SKILL: An Effective Opinion Paragraph |
| --- |
| 1. Begin with a strong topic sentence that clearly states your point of view. |
| 2. Support your opinion by giving good, logical reasons for it. |
| 3. End with a brief conclusion related to the opinion and reasons you gave. |

**A colorful float in a Samba School Parade at Carnival in Brazil**

**D** Read the paragraph about holiday customs. What is the author's opinion?

Old holiday customs are an important connection to our past and our culture, so we should not forget them. These days many people would rather forget some holidays and their celebrations because they want to create new ones, or because they want to feel their life is different from their family's life in the past. They want to focus on the future, not the past, and they think some holiday customs are old fashioned. But the old celebrations are as important as new ones; they are part of our culture and our history, so they are a part of us. It is important to remember them.

**E** Look at the Writing Skill again. Identify the parts of the opinion paragraph in **D**.

1. Circle the topic sentence.

2. Underline the supporting reasons. How many reasons does the author give to support her opinion?

3. Circle the conclusion.

**F** Choose one of the statements from **B**. What is your opinion about it? Brainstorm ideas and complete the visual map with ideas for each part of the paragraph.

| Topic sentence | |
| Supporting reasons | |
| Conclusion | |

**G** Write a paragraph about your opinion. Be sure the paragraph contains all three elements from the Writing Skill.

**GOAL CHECK** Share Opinions about Holidays

1. In small groups, explain your opinions about the sentences in **B** that you chose.

2. Do you agree or disagree with each other's opinions? Tell the class.

> We agree about the first one. New holidays don't feel real!

> I agree, they are like fake holidays!

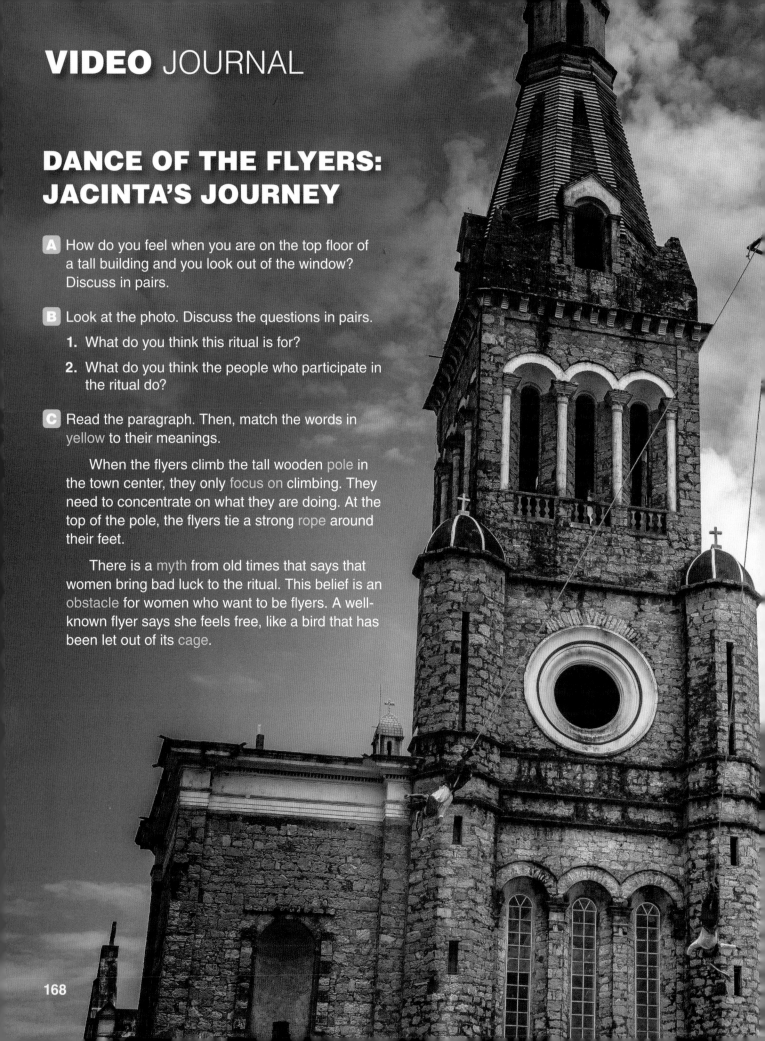

# VIDEO JOURNAL

## DANCE OF THE FLYERS: JACINTA'S JOURNEY

**A** How do you feel when you are on the top floor of a tall building and you look out of the window? Discuss in pairs.

**B** Look at the photo. Discuss the questions in pairs.

1. What do you think this ritual is for?
2. What do you think the people who participate in the ritual do?

**C** Read the paragraph. Then, match the words in yellow to their meanings.

When the flyers climb the tall wooden pole in the town center, they only focus on climbing. They need to concentrate on what they are doing. At the top of the pole, the flyers tie a strong rope around their feet.

There is a myth from old times that says that women bring bad luck to the ritual. This belief is an obstacle for women who want to be flyers. A well-known flyer says she feels free, like a bird that has been let out of its cage.

1. pole _____
2. focus on _____
3. rope _____
4. myth _____
5. obstacle _____
6. cage _____

a. an ancient story that isn't necessarily true

b. a small space with bars on the sides where people keep animals or birds

c. a difficulty

d. a long, thin stick of wood or metal standing straight up in the ground

e. strong, thick string made of long, twisted threads

f. think about

**D** Watch the video. Answer the questions.

1. Who is Jacinta?

_____

2. What does the Dance of the Flyers involve?

_____

3. What is the Dance of the Flyers ritual for?

_____

**E** Watch the video again. Circle **T** for *true* or **F** for *false*.

1. Jacinta was 18 when she first participated in the ritual.    **T   F**

2. When she first climbed, the pole was 50 meters high.    **T   F**

3. Her family has always supported her decision to be a flyer.    **T   F**

4. Some people believe there will be an accident if a woman participates.    **T   F**

5. The flyers go around the pole 15 times when they come down.    **T   F**

**F** Answer the questions. Watch the video again if necessary.

1. What did Jacinta feel the first time she flew?

_____

2. How does she feel when she climbs the pole now?

_____

3. Why does Jacinta say she knows she will go up but she never knows if she will come down?

_____

4. What do these two ideas refer to?

   a. "I had a really cold bar of ice in my stomach."

   _____

   b. "I don't feel like a bird in a cage."

   _____

5. Why is the dance of the flyers also a ritual to Mother Nature?

_____

6. What does Jacinta's family think about her now?

_____

**G** Discuss the questions in pairs.

1. Why do you think Jacinta feels proud of herself?

2. How do you think the ritual has changed from ancient times to now? Will it change in the future? Use the ideas in the box to help you.

costumes   gods   men   safety   women

# Grammar Reference

## UNIT 1

### Lesson A

| Simple Present vs. Present Continuous | |
|---|---|
| Use the simple present to talk about habits and things that are generally true. | I almost never **buy** fruit at the supermarket. **My father** usually **goes** to the farmers' market. |
| Use the present continuous to talk about actions and events that are happening now. Note that you can use contractions. | We **are making** a healthy dinner today. I**'m preparing** a salad with lots of fresh vegetables. |
| Form the present continuous with the correct form of *be (not)* + the *-ing* form of the verb. | My dad **is making** lunch. He **is not making** breakfast. |
| **Yes / No Questions:** | |
| Simple present: *Do / Does* + subject + base form of the verb

Present continuous: correct form of *be* + subject + verb + *-ing* | **Does** she **eat** meat? Yes, she **does**. **Are** you ready to have breakfast? Yes, I **am**. **Is** he **making** a cake? No, he isn't. **Are** they **eating**? Yes, they **are**. |
| **Wh- Questions:** | |
| Simple present: *Wh-* question word + *do / does* + subject + base form of the verb | **What do** you **eat** on special occasions? |
| Present continuous: *Wh-* question word + correct form of *be* + subject + verb + *-ing* | **What are** you **making?** |

**A** Circle the correct form.

1. *Do you buy* / *Are you buying* the ingredients for the dish right now?
2. We always *eat* / *are eating* pozole on special occasions.
3. I almost never *drink* / *am drinking* coffee.
4. *Is dad making* / *Does dad make* a cake because it's my birthday today?
5. We *don't usually go* / *aren't usually going* out for dinner.

**B** Write the correct form of the verb in parentheses.

1. Lila never _____ meat or fish. She's a vegetarian. (eat)
2. What _____? It smells good! (you make)

**170** Grammar Reference

3. I never _____ my cell phone when I'm at the table with my family. (use)
4. My little brother _____ to try new foods. (not like)
5. Right now, I _____ how to make curry. My aunt _____ me. (learn; teach)

**C** Answer the questions.

1. How often do you go out for dinner?

_____

_____

2. Do you usually cook the meals in your house?

_____

_____

3. What are you studying right now?

_____

_____

### Lesson C

| The Simple Past | |
|---|---|
| Use the simple past to talk about completed past actions or situations. | We **walked** to the restaurant last night. The meal **was** delicious. |
| Many verbs are regular in the simple past. They have an *-ed* ending. For regular verbs ending in *-y*, change *y* to *i*, then add *-ed*. For a regular verb that ends in a single vowel and a single consonant, double the consonant, then add *-ed*. | walk - walked prepare - prepared watch - watched plan - pla**nn**ed stop - sto**pp**ed carry - carr**ied** |
| Many common verbs are irregular in the simple past. be - was / were   break - broke   bring - brought   buy - bought   choose - chose   come - came   drink - drank   drive - drove   eat - ate   go - went   have - had   read - read   say - said   see - saw   tell - told | |
| **Negative Statements** | |
| *be*: was / were + not (*wasn't* / *weren't*) Other verbs: *did + not* (*didn't*) + base form | I **was not** (**wasn't**) thirsty. We **did not** (**didn't**) **eat** at home yesterday. |
| **Yes / No questions with *be*:** *Was / Were* **Yes / No questions with other verbs:** *Did* **Wh- Questions:** question word + *did* + subject + base form | **Was** the fish good at the restaurant? **Did** you **go** to the market last Sunday? **Where did** you **have** lunch yesterday? |

**A** Write the correct form of the verb in parentheses.

1. I _____ dinner at my friend's house last night. (have)

2. What _____ at the grocery store this morning? (you buy)

3. Saul _____ lunch. He _____ hungry. (not eat; not be)

4. The restaurant _____ at 1:00 a.m. last night. The wait staff _____ very tired. (close; be)

5. The chef _____ the meat yesterday. (not order)

6. When I _____ to this market last weekend, the fruit _____ very fresh. (come; be)

**B** Complete the questions. Then, write your answers.

1. Where _____ you _____ last Saturday? (go) _____
_____

2. Did _____ your friends there? (see) _____
_____

3. What _____ there? (do)
_____
_____
_____

4. _____ there? (eat)
_____
_____
_____

5. _____?
(your idea) _____
_____

# UNIT 2

## Lesson A

| The Present Perfect vs. The Simple Past | |
|---|---|
| Form the present perfect with the correct form of the verb *have (not)* + past participle of the verb. Note that you can use contractions. | I **have traveled** in Europe. She **has been** a teacher for five years. He**'s visited** the US many times. I **haven't been** to the US. |
| For the past participle of regular verbs, add *-ed* to the base form. | carry - carried    visit - visited    work - worked |
| Some verbs have irregular past participles. | be - been    become - become    eat - eaten    drink - drunk    know - known    take - taken |

| Yes / No Questions: | |
|---|---|
| *Has / Have* + subject + past participle of the verb | **Have** you ever **eaten** tacos? Yes, I **have**. |
| Time expressions we often use with the present perfect: *for* and *since* | We've known each other **for 10 years**. We've known each other **since 2010**. |
| Time expressions we often use with the simple past: *ago* *last week / month / year* *in* + month / year *on* + day or date | We met **10 years ago**. We had dinner together **last month**. We took a trip together **in June**. / **in 2017**. We had dinner **on Friday night**. |

**A** Circle the correct form.

1. We *ate / have eaten* at this restaurant last week.

2. They *took / have taken* several trips together since 2018.

3. I *went / have gone* on vacation in July.

4. He *started / has started* his new job a week ago.

5. *Did she live / Has she lived* in Canada since she was a child?

**B** Write the correct form of the verb in parentheses.

1. Juan and Jorge _____ two years ago in college. (meet)

2. They _____ English for two years and are in the same class this year. (study)

3. Last year, they _____ a trip to London. (take)

4. They _____ to Canada, but they would like to go next year. (never be)

## Lesson C

| Present Perfect Signal Words: *Already, Yet, Ever, and Never* | |
|---|---|
| *Already* and *(not) yet* emphasize that an action has (or has not) happened. | We**'ve already finished** this unit. |
| Use *already* in affirmative statements and questions. | Has class **already started**? No, it **hasn't**. |
| Use *(not) yet* in negative statements and questions. | I **haven't read** that book **yet**. **Has** class **started yet**? No, **not yet**. |

| | |
|---|---|
| Use *never / (not) ever* to talk about something that has or has not happened at any time in the past. | |
| For questions, use *ever*. | **Have** you **ever studied** Chinese? |
| For negative statements, use *never / not ever*. | **I've never learned** to play a musical instrument.<br>She **hasn't ever failed** an exam. |

**A** Complete the conversation with *already, yet, ever,* or *never.*

**Karla:** Have you finished the video project (1) _____?

**Daniel:** Yes, I did it (2) _____. I worked on it all weekend.

**Karla:** Have you (3) _____ done a project like this before?

**Daniel:** No, I haven't (4) _____ done homework like this. Have you?

**Karla:** No, I've (5) _____ done a video project. And I haven't started it (6) _____!

# UNIT 3

## Lesson A

| Future with *Will* | |
|---|---|
| Use *will (not)* + base form of the verb to talk about the future. Note that you can use contractions. | Cities **will be** noisier in the future.<br>There **won't be** more traffic in the future.<br>**I'll move** to the suburbs next year. |
| **Yes / No Questions:**<br>*Will* + base form of the verb<br>**Wh- Questions:**<br>*Wh-* question word + *will* + base form of the verb | **Will** the number of vehicles **continue** to grow? No, it **won't**.<br>**How will** people **move** around the city? |

**A** Unscramble the words to make statements and questions.

1. improve / public / will / transportation

   _____.

2. jobs / there / will / more / be / or fewer / in the future

   _____?

3. future / we / learn / how / in / will / the / languages

   _____?

4. won't / technology / everything / control

   _____

5. free / will / internet / for everyone / be / the

   _____.

**B** Complete the statements and questions about cities in the future. Use *will / won't* and your own ideas.

1. My city _____

   _____.

2. _____

   _____ crowded?

3. _____ pedestrians

   _____.

4. _____

   _____

   vehicles and traffic problems.

5. _____

   _____

   in neighborhoods?

## Lesson C

| Will + Time Clauses | |
|---|---|
| A time clause can be the first or second clause in a sentence. If the time clause is first, it is followed by a comma. Use the simple present in each time clause. | I'll move to the city, **as soon as I graduate**. **Before I move to the city**, I'll look for a job. **After I get a job**, I'll look for an apartment. I'll need a roommate **when I find an apartment**. |
| **Yes / No Questions:**<br>*Will* + subject + base form of the verb + time expression + subject + simple present verb | **Will** you **rent** an apartment **when you move** to the city? |
| **Wh- Questions:**<br>*Wh-* question word + will + subject + base form of the verb + time expression + subject + simple present verb | What **will** you **do after you graduate**? |

**A** Which action will happen first? Write *1* and *2*.

1. Before they open the new park (_____), they will finish the play area (_____).

2. When they improve public transportation (_____), more people will use it (_____).

3. There will be less traffic (_____) after they open the new subway (_____).

4. As soon as I move to the suburbs (_____), I'll buy a bicycle (_____).

5. Will you move to a bigger house (_____) when you have more money (_____)?

# UNIT 4

## Lesson A

| The Comparative, Superlative, and Equative | |
|---|---|
| Comparative adjectives: Add -er to adjectives with 1 or 2 syllables. Use more / less with adjectives of 3 or more syllables. | Doing exercise with a friend is **nicer than** doing exercise alone. Playing sports is **more enjoyable than** going to the gym. Exercise is **less important than** sleep. |
| Superlative adjectives: Use the and add -est to adjectives with 1 or 2 syllables. Use the most / the least with adjectives of 3 or more syllables. | Hana is **the strongest** player on the team. Getting enough sleep is **the most difficult** thing for me. Eating healthy food is **the least difficult** thing for me. |
| To describe people or things that are (or aren't) the same as each other, use (not) as + adjective + as | Eating healthy food is **as important as** doing exercise. For me, doing exercise at the gym is **not as enjoyable as** going for a run. |
| For adjectives ending in -y, change y to i and add -er / -est. | Walking is **easier than** running. My mom is **the healthiest** person in my family. |

**A** Write the correct form of the adjective in parentheses.

1. Sitting down all day is as _____ as eating too much sugar. (harmful)

2. Not doing exercise is _____ than not getting enough sleep. (serious)

3. Walking is _____ form of exercise. (healthy)

4. Spending time with family and friends is _____ than we think. (important)

5. Eating a fruit or vegetable snack is _____ option if you are hungry between meals. (good)

**B** Compare the activities in the box. Use comparatives, superlatives, and equatives.

> baseball   jogging   tennis   a workout   yoga

1. _____
   _____

2. _____
   _____

3. _____
   _____

4. _____
   _____

5. _____
   _____

## Lesson C

| Infinitive of Purpose | |
|---|---|
| The infinitive of purpose gives the reason for doing something: (in order) to + the base form of a verb | You should drink a liter of water a day **to help** your body stay healthy. Take vitamin C (**in order**) **to avoid** getting a cold. |
| The infinitive of purpose can come in the beginning or in the middle of a sentence. When it begins the sentence, it is followed by a comma. | **To stop hiccups**, I drink a glass of water. **In order to stay healthy**, I take vitamins every day. |

**A** Correct the mistake in each sentence.

1. In order lose weight, you should eat less sugar.

2. You should do more exercise to being healthier.

3. To avoid stress I do yoga every day.

4. Drink honey and lemon help a sore throat.

**B** Give a reason for each action. Add a comma when necessary.

1. I do exercise every day.
   _____

2. I listen to classical music when I drive.
   _____

3. I don't eat sugar.
   _____

4. I cycle to school.
   _____

# UNIT 5

## Lesson A

### Past Continuous and Simple Past

| | |
|---|---|
| Use the past continuous to talk about something that was in progress at a specific time in the past. | She **was preparing** for the marathon all last month. |
| Use the simple past with the past continuous to say that something happened when another event was in progress. | She **was preparing** for the marathon when she **broke** her leg. |
| **Past Continuous:** <br> Subject + *was (not)* / *were (not)* + *-ing* form of a verb. Note that you can use contractions. <br><br> **Yes / No Questions:** <br> *Was* / *Were* + subject + *-ing* form of a verb. <br><br> **Wh- Questions:** <br> *Wh-* question word + *was* / *were* + subject + *-ing* form of a verb. | The students **were practicing** their reading skills. <br> They **weren't talking**. <br><br> **Was** the teacher **listening** to them? <br><br> **What were** they **reading**? |
| We usually use *when* for the action in the simple past and *while* for the action in the past continuous. | She was preparing for the marathon **when she broke** her leg. <br> She broke her leg **while she was preparing** for the marathon. |
| Use a comma after a time clause when it begins a sentence. | **While they were climbing**, one of the men fell. |
| Only action verbs are used with the past continuous. <br> Stative verbs (e.g., like, understand, know) are not used in the past continuous. | Sam **was dealing with** some challenges at work last year. He often **seemed** upset. |

**A** Circle the correct form.

1. We *dealt* / *were dealing* with a difficult situation at work when the boss *left* / *was leaving* suddenly.
2. My friend *convinced* / *was convincing* me to run the marathon with her. I *started* / *was starting* training today.
3. While she *traveled* / *was traveling*, she *met* / *was meeting* a lot of interesting people.
4. The team *knew* / *were knowing* how to prepare for the challenge.
5. I *achieved* / *was achieving* my goal of becoming healthier. I now weigh less, and I exercise every day.

**B** Write the correct past form of the verbs in parentheses.

1. Although the teacher _____ very fast, I _____ the class. (speak; understand)
2. The runner _____ good progress when she _____ her ankle. (make; hurt)
3. As soon as I _____ the finish line, I _____ I could achieve my goal. (see; know)
4. The storm _____ while we _____ to leave. (begin; prepare)

## Lesson C

### Enough, Not Enough, Too + Adjective

| | |
|---|---|
| Use adjective + *enough* to say something is the necessary amount. | She's 18. She's **old enough** to drive a car. |
| Use *not* + adjective + *enough* to say it is less than necessary. | She's 15. She's **not** / she isn't **old enough** to drive a car. |
| Use *too* + adjective to say it is more than necessary. | She's 15, she's **too young** to drive a car. |
| **Yes / No Questions:** <br> Correct form of *be* + subject + adjective + *enough* + *to* infinitive | **Are you old enough** to drive? |

**A** Unscramble the words to make statements and questions.

1. run / enough / I'm / to / strong / not / a marathon

   _____.

2. this movie / old / are / enough / watch / you / to

   _____?

3. to / tall / play / enough / basketball / he's / not

   _____.

**4.** expensive / the trip / too / is

_____.

**5.** fast / win the race / she / enough / is / to

_____?

# UNIT 6

## Lesson A

| The Past Perfect | |
|---|---|
| The past perfect is used to describe a past event that happened before another point in the past, or to explain why a past event or situation happened. | When I graduated from college, I **had** already **started** working. Max chose to go to France for a semester because he **had** already **studied** French. |
| Form the past perfect with *had (not)* + the past participle of the verb.<br><br>Questions:<br>*Had* + subject + past participle of the verb?<br><br>Adverbs and time expressions with the past perfect:<br>*just*<br>*already*<br>*when*<br>*by the time* | He **had** always **loved** learning languages.<br>I **hadn't graduated** from college when I started working.<br><br>**Had** you already **graduated** when you got your first job? Yes, I **had**.<br><br>I had **just** started college when I got my first job. I started college in September and I started working in November.<br>I had **already** started college when I got my first job.<br>**When** I took the exam, I had prepared well.<br>**By the time** I finished the exam, some students had already left. |

**A** Which action happened first? Write *1* and *2*.

**1.** Susy had just graduated (_____) when she moved to Mexico City (_____).

**2.** By the time Jon went to elementary school (_____), he had already learned to read and write by himself (_____).

**3.** Zara went to Chile on an exchange program (_____) because she had studied Spanish in high school (_____).

**4.** I had known Max for a year (_____) before I realized he spoke four languages (_____).

**B** Write the correct form of the verbs in parentheses.

**1.** I _____ a career in design, but I _____ to change to teaching. (choose; decide)

**2.** The exam _____ when the fire alarm _____. (just start; ring)

**3.** By the time the teacher _____, the students _____ the classroom. (arrive; already leave)

**4.** Lin _____ as a construction worker for 10 years before he _____ an architect. (work; become)

## Lesson C

| Grammar: *How* + Adjective or Adverb | |
|---|---|
| Use *how* to ask a question about a descriptive adjective or adverb.<br><br>With adjectives, use *be*:<br>*How* + adjective + correct form of *be* + subject | **How careful** are you? I've never broken any bones! |
| With adverbs, use other verbs:<br>*How* + adverb + *do / does* + subject + base form of the verb<br>Note that you can also use *can* instead of *do / does*. | **How badly** does he drive? He crashed twice last month.<br>**How fast** can you type? I can type 90 words a minute. |
| Common adjectives: *young, old, early, clean, happy, difficult, polite, serious*<br>Common adverbs: *well, badly, often, rarely, quickly, slowly, easily, carefully* | |

**A** Write questions with the adjectives and adverbs in parentheses. Then, give an answer to the questions like the examples in the chart above.

**1.** How _____ *fast can you* _____ run?
(fast) _____ *I can run a kilometer in 5 minutes.* _____

_____

**2.** How _____?
(happy) _____

_____

**3.** How _____ exercise?
(often) _____

_____

**4.** How _____
play tennis? (well) _____

_____

**5.** How _____
your grandmother? (youthful) _____

# UNIT 7

## Lesson A

### Passive Voice (Present Tense)

| | |
|---|---|
| The passive voice emphasizes the object or receiver of an action.<br>Form the present passive with *is / are* + the past participle of the verb. | A large amount of plastic **is thrown away** every day. |
| Regular past participles add -*ed* to the base form of the verb. | call - called    carry - carried<br>drop - dropped    help - helped<br>laugh - laughed    look - looked<br>stop - stopped    walk - walked<br>worry - worried |
| Many common verbs have irregular past participles. | begin - begun    break - broken<br>bring - brought    buy - bought<br>catch - caught    choose – chosen<br>drive - driven    eat - eaten<br>make - made    see - seen<br>teach - taught    throw - thrown<br>write - written |
| **Yes / No Questions:**<br>*Is / Are* + subject + past participle of the verb<br>**Wh- Questions:**<br>*Wh-* question word + *is / are* + subject + past participle of the verb | **Is** solar energy **used** to heat water? Yes, **it is**.<br><br>**Where are** plastic bottles **recycled**? |

**A** Write the passive form of the verbs from the box.

> recycle    reduce    reuse    teach    throw away

These days, people think more carefully about what they throw away at home. For example, coffee cups and cloth bags (1) _____, and glass bottles, cans, and cardboard (2) _____. Thanks to this, fewer things (3) _____ and the amount of trash (4) _____. People are beginning to change their habits, and it is important that children (5) _____ to think about these things.

## Lesson C

### Passive Voice with *By*

| | |
|---|---|
| Use *by* with the passive voice to emphasize who or what does something (the agent). | The plastic bottles are washed **by powerful machines**.<br>Eco-friendly cars are produced **by several different companies** now. |

**A** Read the sentences and cross out the *by* phrases when they are not necessary.

1. Energy is produced by the solar panels on top of our house.

2. In many countries, a lot of food is wasted by people.

3. Our notebooks are made from recycled paper by factory workers.

4. Eco-friendly cars are powered by electricity, not gasoline.

# UNIT 8

## Lesson A

### Real Conditionals in the Future

| | |
|---|---|
| Use the real conditional for situations that can happen in the future:<br>*if* + subject + simple present verb (the condition), + subject + *will / be going to* + base form of the verb (the result) | **If we don't control** pollution, more sea animals **will become** extinct.<br>Plastic straws **are going to hurt** more sea turtles **if we keep** throwing them away. |
| The condition or the result can come first. Use a comma after the condition when it comes first. | **If we tell** people about the problems, they **will change** their habits.<br>People **will change** their habits **if we tell** them about the problems. |
| **Yes / No Questions:**<br>*Will* + subject + base form of the verb + *if* + subject + simple present verb.<br>**Wh- Questions:**<br>*Wh-* question word + *will / be going to* + subject + the base form of the verb + *if* + subject + simple present verb. | **Will** our planet **survive** if temperatures **continue** to increase? No, it **won't**.<br><br>**What is going to happen** if temperatures **continue** to increase? |

**A** Circle the correct form.

1. Many animals *become / will become* extinct if we *don't protect / will protect* them.

2. If we *recycle / are going to recycle* more, there *is / is going to be* less trash.

3. Wild animals *lose / will lose* their habitat if we *build / will build* factories outside the city.

4. More species *disappear / will disappear* if we *continue / will continue* to pollute the oceans.

5. What *happen / will happen* if future generations *don't save / will save* the environment?

**B** Write the correct form of the verbs in the box.

> be   change   have   help   increase
> protect   stop   take care   understand   use

1. If you _____ using plastic bags for your shopping, you _____ the environment.

2. The climate _____ more if temperatures _____.

3. If more people _____ public transportation, there _____ less traffic in the city.

4. Our children _____ a better future if we _____ of the planet now.

5. If our children _____ conservation, they _____ nature for the future.

## Lesson C

| Quantifiers | |
|---|---|
| **With count nouns, use:** | |
| *too few* (not enough) *a few* (a small number) *some* (not a small or large number) *a lot of / many* (a large number) *too many* (more than necessary) | There are **too few conservation programs**. There are **a few animal protection centers**. We need **some volunteers** to help. The center has **a lot of volunteers**. There are **too many endangered species**. |
| **With non-count nouns, use:** | |
| *too little* (not enough) *a little* (a small amount) *some* (not a small or large amount) *a lot of* (a large amount) *too much* (more than necessary) | There is **too little money** for the project. There is **a little money** to pay the volunteers. The center gets **some help** from the government. We need **a lot of food** for the animals. We have **too much** work. |

**A** Write the correct quantifier: *too few / too little, too many / too much, a few / a little*.

1. The rescue center has _____ vets. It needs more.

2. There is _____ education about the environment. Schools need to teach children how to protect our wildlife.

3. There are _____ orphaned animals. The center is too small to take them all.

4. There are _____ volunteers, but we need more.

5. We have _____ milk for the baby chimpanzees, but it is not enough.

# UNIT 9

## Lesson A

| Used to | |
|---|---|
| Use *used to* + base form of the verb to show how things have changed from the past to the present, and to talk about past habits. Note that we sometimes use *always* with *used to* to talk about habits. | People **used to travel** by horse and cart. We **used to communicate** by letters, now we use cell phones for most of our communication. I **used to eat** meat every day, now I only eat it two or three times a week. I always **used to drive** to work, now I bike. |
| **Negative Statements:** *didn't* + *use to* + base form of the verb | People didn't **use to worry** about the environment. |
| **Yes / No Questions:** *Did* + subject + *use to* + base form of the verb **Wh- Questions:** *Wh-* question word + *did* + subject + *use to* + base form of the verb | **Did** your family **use to recycle**? No, we didn't. **Did** you **use to write** letters? Yes, we did. **What kind of houses did** people **use to live** in? |

**A** Circle the correct form.

1. Long distance travel *use to / used to* take longer than it takes today.

2. Why did travel *use to / used to* be so challenging in the past?

3. In the past, there didn't *use to / used to* be as many opportunities for trade as there are nowadays.

4. How did people *use to / used to* buy things before money existed?

5. Before trade with China began, people didn't *use to / used to* wear silk clothes.

**B** Complete the questions and statements with the correct form of *use to* and your own ideas.

1. Before we had cell phones,
   _____
   _____ .

2. I _____
   (negative), but now _____
   _____ .

3. How _____
   _____ ?

4. Why _____
   _____ ?

5. I _____
   _____ . (negative)

6. People _____
   _____ .

## Lesson C

| Passive Voice (Past Tense) | |
|---|---|
| The passive voice emphasizes the object or receiver of an action in the past. Use *by* when you want to say who or what did something (the agent). Form the past passive with *was / were* + the past participle of the verb. | A large number of plastic bags **were used** every day, but now people use reusable bags. A lot of plastic bags **were used by** shoppers at supermarkets. |
| Regular past participles add *–ed* to the base form of the verb. | believe - believed    include - included    happen - happened    like - liked    listen - listened    provide - provided    support - supported    wonder - wondered |
| Many common verbs have irregular past participles. | build - built    cut - cut    draw - drawn    find - found    fly- flown    forget - forgotten    freeze - frozen    hide - hidden    lose - lost    sell - sold    spend - spent    steal - stolen    win - won |
| **Yes / No Questions:** Was / Were + subject + past participle of the verb | **Was** coal **used** for heating in the past? Yes, **it was**. |
| **Wh- Questions:** Wh- question word + was / were + subject + past participle of the verb | **How was** coal **delivered** to people's houses? |

**A** Write the correct form of the verbs in parentheses.

1. Large stones _____ to build the Egyptian pyramids. (use)
2. In the past, igloos _____ from blocks of ice by the Inuit people. (build)
3. In other countries, houses _____ from mud and dry grass in the past. (make)
4. Before paper _____, people used to write on wood and dried animal skin. (invent)
5. Paper _____ to Europe until the 11th century. (not bring)

**B** Use the correct form of the past passive of the verbs in the box to complete the questions and statements.

> allow   change   invent   lose   make

1. When _____ money _____?
2. In the past, girls (not) _____ to go to school.
3. How _____ clothes _____ in the past?
4. Communication _____ completely by the invention of the internet.
5. Luckily, traditions (not) _____ when the Sami people moved to towns.

# UNIT 10

## Lesson A

| Expressing Necessity | |
|---|---|
| Use *must* + base form of the verb in writing and formal speaking to say that something is an obligation or a rule. | Visitors **must have** a visa to enter the country. |
| Use *have to* or *need to* + base form of the verb in informal speaking to say that something is necessary (but not an obligation or a rule). | We **have to buy** our tickets. Danny **needs to get** a new suitcase for the trip. |
| Use *have got to* + base form of the verb for more emphasis. Note that you can use contractions. | David **has got to make** a hotel reservation soon! He**'s got to** call the hotel today. |
| Use *don't have to / don't need to* + base form of the verb to say that something is not necessary. | They **don't need to make** a reservation, it's not busy. |

| Yes / No Questions: | |
|---|---|
| *Do / Does* + subject + *have to / need to* + base form of the verb | **Do** you **need to get** a visa for Canada? Yes, **I do**. **Does** Ivan **have to renew** his passport? No, **he doesn't**. |
| **Wh- Questions:** | |
| *Wh-* question word + *do / does* + subject + *have to / need to* + base form of the verb | **What do** you **have to do** at check-in? **When do** you **need to be** at the boarding gate? We **had to show** our passports at check-in. Someone **will need to** help Lin with her carry-on bag. She's hurt her arm. **Did** you **have to get** a visa? Yes, I did. **Where did** you **need to change** trains? |
| Note that *have to* and *need to* can be used with different verb forms. | |

**A** Circle the correct form.

1. When you get to the airport, you *need to / must* check the weight of your bags.
2. Did Luisa *have to / must* check any baggage?
3. All travelers *must / need to* go through the airport security check.
4. You *need to / must* show your passport on arrival.
5. Travelers don't *have to / must* check their carry-on bag.

**B** Write 5 things you and your family or friends need to (or don't need to) do to prepare for a trip. Use *have to / need to*.

1. _____
   _____.
2. _____
   _____.
3. _____
   _____.
4. _____
   _____.
5. _____
   _____.

## Lesson C

**Expressing Prohibition**

| Use the negative form of *must* to say that something is prohibited: *must not* + base form of the verb. | You **must not smoke** on board an airplane. |
|---|---|

| Note that you can use contractions. For other tenses, use *had to / will have to*. | You **mustn't take** a bottle of water in your carry-on. They **had to have** a health check-up to get their visas. |
|---|---|
| We can also use *can't* + base form of the verb to say that something is not allowed. | You **can't take** a large piece of baggage as carry-on. |
| *Must not* is stronger than *can't* and is used for rules. | The government said visitors **must not overstay** their visas. The airline said passengers **can't board** an international flight without a visa. |

**A** Correct the mistake in each sentence.

1. You can't to use the bathroom while the plane is taking off or landing.
2. When I traveled to India last month, I must get a visa.
3. All travelers must to show their passport and boarding pass to be able to board the plane.
4. You will must renew your passport before you travel next month.

**B** Write 5 things someone visiting your country needs to know. Use *have to / need to / must / must not / can't*.

1. _____
   _____.
2. _____
   _____.
3. _____
   _____.
4. _____
   _____.
5. _____
   _____.

# UNIT 11

## Lesson A

**Modals for Giving Advice**

| Use *should (not)* + verb to say that something is (or isn't) a good idea. | You **should choose** a career that fits your personality. You **shouldn't apply** for an office job if you don't like to be inside all day. |
|---|---|

| | |
|---|---|
| Use *had better (not)* to say that something bad could happen if the advice isn't followed. Note that you can use contractions. | You **had better prepare** well for your interview. He**'d better not fail** the exam. |
| We can also use *ought to* + base form of the verb to give advice. *Ought to* is more formal than *should* and *had better*. | The government **ought to give** more scholarships for students to study abroad. |
| Use *maybe, perhaps,* or *I think* with modals to make the advice sound gentler and friendlier. | **Maybe** you **should become** a health care worker. |

**A** Complete the letter with *should, shouldn't, had better,* or *ought to.*

Dear Reader,

I am happy you asked me for advice. If you want to become an innovator, you (1) _____ think about a problem you want to solve.
Since there are lots of problems in the world, it (2) _____ be too hard! Remember, it takes a long time to solve a problem well, so you (3) _____ be patient.

Sincerely,

The Career Advisor

**B** Your friend has an important job interview. Give him or her advice. Use *should, shouldn't, had better,* or *ought to,* and the ideas in the box to help you.

clothes        English        experience
preparation    questions

1. _____
   _____.
2. _____
   _____.
3. _____
   _____.
4. _____
   _____.
5. _____
   _____.

## Lesson C

### Indefinite Pronouns

| | |
|---|---|
| Indefinite pronouns refer to unspecified nouns. | **Somebody** was with the career advisor when I went to see her. (I don't know who it was.) |
| To talk about an entire group of nouns: *everybody / everyone / everything / everywhere* | **Everyone** went to the meeting. The boss wanted to talk to all of us. **Everything** in the book is important. You need to study all of it. |
| To talk about none of a group of nouns: *nobody / no one / nothing / nowhere* | I want to sell my computer, but **no one** I know wants to buy it. There is **nowhere** interesting to visit in my town. |
| To talk about an unspecified noun: *somebody / someone / something / somewhere* | You should talk to **someone** at the career advising center. (I don't know who specifically.) It is good to do **something** as a volunteer. (I don't know what.) |
| To emphasize that it's not important to specify a certain person, place, or thing: *anybody / anyone / anything / anywhere* | You need work experience. **Anything** you do will be helpful. (It doesn't matter what it is.) You can work **anywhere**. (It doesn't matter where.) |
| Negative statements and questions: *anybody / anyone / anything / anywhere* | I don't know **anybody** in the office. Do you know **anything** about the job? |

**A** Circle the correct indefinite pronouns.

1. An inventor is *nobody / somebody* who is interested in problem solving.
2. Many scientists and engineers are trying to do *something / anything* to solve the problems of the world.
3. But it is not only these professionals. Ordinary people around the world have developed innovations in their communities with almost *nothing / something*.
4. *Everybody / Nobody* wants to make the world a better place.
5. I hope to do *something / anything* important with my life.

**B** Complete the sentences with indefinite pronouns.

1. Is there _____ I should know before the interview?
2. They will want to know _____ about

your volunteer experience, but don't tell them all your crazy stories!

3. I'm nervous— _____ told me that the interview is very challenging.

4. Does _____ know what the salary will be for this job? Who can I ask?

5. Will there be opportunities to travel _____ with this job?

# UNIT 12

## Lesson A

### Comparisons with *as... as*

| | |
|---|---|
| Use subject + *be* + *as* + adjective + *as* + complement to say that two things are equal. | Halloween **is as interesting as** Day of the Dead. They are both celebrations that people enjoy. |
| Note that you can use contractions. | Halloween**'s as interesting as** Day of the Dead. |
| Use subject + *be* + *not as* + adjective + *as* + complement to say that two things are not equal. | A music festival **is not as interesting as** the Burning Man festival. I like the art at Burning Man.<br>New Year's Eve **isn't as noisy as** Carnival. |
| **Questions:** | |
| Correct form of *be* + subject + *as* + adjective + *as* + complement | **Is** your birthday **as exciting as** other holidays? |

**A** Correct the mistake in each sentence.

1. Day of the Dead is as well known than Halloween around the world.

2. For children, Three Kings' Day is most exciting as Christmas.

3. The New Year's crowd in Trafalgar Square, London, is as bigger as the crowd in Times Square, New York.

4. The traditions in one culture are as important the traditions in another culture.

5. Old celebrations are as more important as new celebrations.

**B** Choose two places to visit in your city or country. Compare them using *(not) as...as*.

1. _____
_____.

2. _____
_____.

3. _____
_____.

4. _____
_____.

5. _____
_____.

## Lesson C

### *Would rather*

| | |
|---|---|
| Use *would rather (not)* + base form of the verb to talk about actions we prefer. Note that you can use contractions. | **I would rather have** a small party than a big party for my birthday.<br>**I'd rather go out** for dinner.<br>**I'd rather not cook** tonight. |
| Use *one* to avoid repeating the noun. | **I would rather have** a small party than a big **one** for my birthday. |
| **Questions:** | |
| *Would you rather* + base form of verb + complement | **Would you rather eat** out tonight or **stay** home?<br>**Would you rather go** straight home? |
| *Wh-* question word + *would you rather* + base form + complement | **How would you rather celebrate** your birthday? |

**A** Write statements and questions using the information in parentheses and an appropriate verb.

1. (Carnival or Day of the Dead)
_____
_____?

2. (a restaurant or a coffee shop)
_____
_____.

3. (not – downtown on New Year's Eve)
_____
_____.

4. (birthday) _____
_____?

5. (with family or with friends)
_____
_____?

## Spelling Rules for Verbs Ending in -s and -es

| | |
|---|---|
| 1. Add -s to most verbs. | like-like**s**<br>sit-sit**s** |
| 2. Add -es to verbs that end in -ch, -s, -sh, -x, or -z. | catch-catch**es**<br>miss-miss**es**<br>wash-wash**es**<br>mix-mix**es**<br>buzz-buzz**es** |
| 3. Change the -y to -i and add -es when the base form ends in a consonant + -y. | cry-cr**ies**<br>carry-carr**ies** |
| 4. Do not change the -y when the base form ends in a vowel + -y. | pay-pay**s**<br>stay-stay**s** |
| 5. Some verbs are irregular in the third-person singular -s form of the simple present. | be-**is**<br>go-**goes**<br>do-**does**<br>have-**has** |

## Spelling Rules for Verbs Ending in -ing

| | |
|---|---|
| 1. Add -ing to the base form of most verbs. | eat-eat**ing**<br>do-do**ing**<br>speak-speak**ing**<br>carry-carry**ing** |
| 2. When the verb ends in a consonant + -e, drop the -e and add -ing. | ride-rid**ing**<br>write-writ**ing** |
| 3. For one-syllable verbs that end in a consonant + a vowel + a consonant (CVC), double the final consonant and add -ing.<br><br>Do not double the final consonant for verbs that end in CVC when the final consonant is -w, -x, or -y. | stop-stop**ping**<br>sit-sit**ting**<br><br>show-show**ing**<br>fix-fix**ing**<br>stay-stay**ing** |
| 4. For two-syllable verbs that end in CVC and have stress on the first syllable, add -ing. Do not double the final consonant.<br><br>For two-syllable verbs that end in CVC and have stress on the last syllable, double the final consonant and add -ing. | ENter-enter**ing**<br>LISTen-listen**ing**<br><br>beGIN-begin**ning**<br>ocCUR-occur**ring** |

## Spelling Rules for Verbs Ending in -ed

| | |
|---|---|
| 1. Add -ed to the base form of most verbs that end in a consonant. | start-start**ed**<br>talk-talk**ed** |
| 2. Add -d if the base form of the verb ends in -e. | dance-danc**ed**<br>live-liv**ed** |
| 3. When the base form of the verb ends in a consonant + -y, change the -y to -i and add -ed.<br><br>Do not change the -y to -i when the verb ends in a vowel + -y. | cry-cr**ied**<br>worry-worr**ied**<br><br>stay-stay**ed** |
| 4. For one-syllable verbs that end in a consonant + a vowel + a consonant (CVC), double the final consonant and add -ed.<br><br>Do not double the final consonant of verbs that end in -w, -x, or -y. | stop-stop**ped**<br>rob-rob**bed**<br><br>follow-follow**ed**<br>fix-fix**ed**<br>play-play**ed** |
| 5. For two-syllable verbs that end in CVC and have stress on the first syllable, add -ed. Do not double the final consonant.<br><br>For two-syllable verbs that end in CVC and have stress on the last syllable, double the final consonant and add -ed. | ORder-order**ed**<br>HAPpen-happen**ed**<br><br>ocCUR-occur**red**<br>preFER-prefer**red** |

## Spelling Rules for Comparative and Superlative Forms

|  | Adjective/ Adverb | Comparative | Superlative |
|---|---|---|---|
| 1. Add -er or -est to one-syllable adjectives and adverbs. | tall<br>fast | tall**er**<br>fast**er** | tall**est**<br>fast**est** |
| 2. Add -r or -st to adjectives that end in -e. | nice | nice**r** | nice**st** |
| 3. Change the -y to -i and add -er or -est to two-syllable adjectives and adverbs that end in -y. | easy<br>happy | eas**ier**<br>happ**ier** | eas**iest**<br>happ**iest** |
| 4. Double the final consonant and add -er or -est to one-syllable adjectives or adverbs that end in a consonant + a vowel + a consonant (CVC). | big<br>hot | big**ger**<br>hot**ter** | big**gest**<br>hot**test** |

## Common Irregular Verbs

| Base Form | Simple Past | Past Participle | Base Form | Simple Past | Past Participle |
|---|---|---|---|---|---|
| begin | began | begun | make | made | made |
| break | broke | broken | meet | met | met |
| bring | brought | brought | pay | paid | paid |
| buy | bought | bought | put | put | put |
| come | came | come | read | read | read |
| do | did | done | ride | rode | ridden |
| drink | drank | drunk | run | ran | run |
| drive | drove | driven | say | said | said |
| eat | ate | eaten | see | saw | seen |
| feel | felt | felt | send | sent | sent |
| get | got | gotten | sit | sat | sat |
| give | gave | given | sleep | slept | slept |
| go | went | gone | speak | spoke | spoken |
| have | had | had | swim | swam | swum |
| hear | heard | heard | take | took | taken |
| hurt | hurt | hurt | tell | told | told |
| know | knew | known | think | thought | thought |
| leave | left | left | throw | threw | thrown |
| let | let | let | understand | understood | understood |
| lose | lost | lost | write | wrote | written |

## Phrasal Verbs (Separable) and Their Meanings

*Don't forget to **turn off** the oven before you leave the house.*
*Don't forget to **turn** the oven **off** before you leave the house.*

| Phrasal Verb | Meaning | Example Sentence |
|---|---|---|
| **blow up** | cause something to explode | *The workers **blew** the bridge **up**.* |
| **bring back** | return | *She **brought** the shirt **back** to the store.* |
| **bring up** | 1. raise from childhood<br>2. introduce a topic to discuss | 1. *My grandmother **brought** me **up**.*<br>2. *Don't **bring up** that subject.* |
| **call back** | return a telephone call | *I **called** Rajil **back** but there was no answer.* |
| **call off** | cancel | *They **called** the wedding **off** after their fight.* |
| **cheer up** | make someone feel happier | *Her visit to the hospital **cheered** the patients **up**.* |
| **clear up** | clarify, explain | *She **cleared** the problem **up**.* |
| **do over** | do again | *His teacher asked him to **do** the essay **over**.* |
| **figure out** | solve, understand | *The student **figured** the problem **out**.* |
| **fill in** | complete information | ***Fill in** the answers on the test.* |
| **fill out** | complete an application or form | *I had to **fill** many forms **out** at the doctor's office.* |
| **find out** | learn, uncover | *Did you **find** anything **out** about the new plans?* |
| **give away** | offer something freely | *They are **giving** prizes **away** at the store.* |
| **give back** | return | *The boy **gave** the pen **back** to the teacher.* |
| **give up** | stop doing | *I **gave up** sugar last year. Will you **give** it **up**?* |
| **help out** | aid, support someone | *I often **help** my older neighbors **out**.* |
| **lay off** | dismiss workers from their jobs | *My company **laid** 200 workers **off** last year.* |
| **leave on** | allow a machine to continue working | *I **left** the lights **on** all night.* |
| **let in** | allow someone to enter | *She opened a window to **let** some fresh air **in**.* |
| **look over** | examine | *We **looked** the contract **over** before signing it.* |
| **make up** | say something untrue or fictional (a story, a lie) | *The child **made** the story **up**. It wasn't true at all.* |
| **pay back** | return money, repay a loan | *I **paid** my friend **back**. I owed him $10.* |
| **pick up** | 1. get someone or something<br>2. lift | 1. *He **picked up** his date at her house.*<br>2. *I **picked** the ball **up** and threw it.* |
| **put off** | delay, postpone | *Don't **put** your homework **off** until tomorrow.* |
| **put out** | 1. take outside<br>2. extinguish | 1. *He **put** the trash **out**.*<br>2. *Firefighters **put out** the fire.* |
| **set up** | 1. arrange<br>2. start something | 1. *She **set** the tables **up** for the party.*<br>2. *They **set up** the project.* |
| **shut off** | stop something from working | *Can you **shut** the water **off**?* |
| **sort out** | make sense of something | *We have to **sort** this problem **out**.* |
| **straighten up** | make neat and orderly | *I **straightened** the messy living room **up**.* |
| **take back** | own again | *He **took** the tools that he loaned me **back**.* |
| **take off** | remove | *She **took off** her hat and gloves.* |
| **take out** | remove | *I **take** the trash **out** on Mondays.* |
| **talk over** | discuss a topic until it is understood | *Let's **talk** this plan **over** before we do anything.* |
| **think over** | reflect, ponder | *She **thought** the job offer **over** carefully.* |
| **throw away/<br>throw out** | get rid of something, discard | *He **threw** the old newspapers **away**.*<br>*I **threw out** the old milk in the fridge.* |
| **try on** | put on clothing to see if it fits | *He **tried** the shoes **on** but didn't buy them.* |
| **turn down** | refuse | *His manager **turned** his proposal **down**.* |
| **turn off** | stop something from working | *Can you **turn** the TV **off**, please?* |
| **turn on** | switch on, operate | *I **turned** the lights **on** in the dark room.* |
| **turn up** | increase the volume | ***Turn** the radio **up**, so we can hear the news.* |
| **wake up** | make someone stop sleeping | *The noise **woke** the baby **up**.* |
| **write down** | write on paper | *I **wrote** the information **down**.* |

# Credits